KERBY:

Funny tales from a 1990's Scottish childhood

GRAEME JOHNSTON

Copyright © 2015 Graeme Johnston
Cover art by Bruce Mack

All rights reserved.

ISBN: 1507762674
ISBN-13: 978-1507762677

For Mum, Dad and Jen.

Author's note:
All names have been changed.
You'll soon see why.

Contents

I: WELCOME TO THE TERRORDOME 1

II: DIARY OF A MADMAN 6

III: KISS ME 17

IV: WICKED GAME 29

V: HOME SICK HOME 43

VI: IDIOT BOX 60

VII: CHALK DUST TORTURE 74

VIII: SWEET LIKE CHOCOLATE 98

IX: THE MASSES AGAINST THE CLASSES 106

X: VIRTUAL INSANITY 129

XI: ALL MY BEST FRIENDS ARE METALHEADS 140

XII: TEENAGE RIOT 164

XIII: MY FAVOURITE GAME 171

XIV: THIS IS HARDCORE 191

XV: GUILTY CONSCIENCE 197

XVI: ORIGINAL PRANKSTER 204

XVII: THE FULL MONTY 219

XVIII: UP IN THE SKY 225

XIX: THE END OF THE INNOCENCE 237

Winding our way through the Irish countryside one pothole at a time, we made our approach towards yet another hilly horizon on the seemingly endless backroad. As the driver, Mum was becoming increasingly anxious about our being lost.

All she wanted at that moment was for the two of us to roll over the brow of this latest horizon and discover an end in sight; a junction joining a better class of road, a road sign, anything to put an end to this horrible, pock-marked track. She was visibly dejected when our car mounted the hill to reveal yet more snaking road and another distant horizon.

We were in rural County Sligo; where exactly, we couldn't say. Following signs for County Donegal (and the holiday home in which we were spending this miserable week), it became clear that we had accidentally strayed from the beaten path.

'I knew I shoulda taken that left turn at Albuquerque...'

We had ended up on some poorly-maintained minor road along which houses were sporadically dotted at infrequent intervals; each house sat back from the road, to be reached by its own little farm track. As one of the most sparsely populated countries in Europe, areas of countryside like this are very common in the Republic of Ireland.

We were lost and there was no sign of life, no one who could send us on our way again.

Worse still, I had just started feeling intense pangs in my stomach; I looked at the distant horizon, and hoped they were only from hunger...

I: WELCOME TO THE TERRORDOME

It remains the only time I've ever had my erect penis out in the middle of a supermarket. I don't have any plans to repeat the stunt, but never say never.

The scene played out one day in the late 1980s, on a family trip to Tesco in Irvine to do that week's 'big shop'.

My mum had that red-faced, bedraggled look worn only by young mothers after an hour of food shopping with a three- and four-year old in tow. My dad bore the stress of this somewhat better, with his already-receding hair not long or thick enough to have been matted into his sweaty, anxious forehead in the same way my mum's had.

Parenthood brings with it many trials and tribulations.

You learn to disarm stressful situations by dreaming up cheesy songs *. You make peace with urinating becoming a spectator sport. Tea is always enjoyed stone cold, and you master functioning with a sleep pattern that can involve seeing every hour on the clock.

* My wife's most impressive feat was taking the tune of Beyonce's *Single Ladies* and turning the act of applying Sudacrem onto our screaming son's red bottom into a jolly song of 'If you liked it then you should have put some cream on it, whoa oh oh!'

As yet, however, no parent has found the secret to unloading a full shopping trolley **and** successfully supervising their infant kids.

The seats built into the front of the trolley provide a great solution for approximately forty five seconds, or until restlessness sets in.

Of course, another answer is for one parent to unload items onto the checkout conveyer belt while the other parent deals with any offspring. Here, the problem arises as soon as a second child is brought into the mix. One parent, two children, a supermarket full of hiding spots and aisles stocked with tampons and condoms. What could possibly go wrong?

My mum managed a bemused smile at the grinning checkout assistant's stifled chuckles. Hearing more laughter in the queues around her, she turned to frown inquisitively at my dad, every inch the picture of confusion himself.

One look over his shoulder clued them into the source of everyone's amusement. Their son, a three year old me, had exposed himself to reveal a 'baby boner'.

(Surprisingly common, this is one of the most terrifying and bewildering phenomenon that new parents are charged with accepting – apparently infants will, on occasion, develop pointless erections.)

I was stood there in the middle of Tesco, trousers and pants at the ankles, blowing on my boner.

'GRAEME!' my mum screamed, scarlet with embarrassment. 'What in God's name are you doing?!'

'I'm blowin' on it, Mum!' I replied. 'Hot willy! Hot willy!'

At that, I went back to blowing on my penis, to the amusement of everyone but my parents.

Years later, probably after a suitable amount of therapy, this became one of their choice stories to trot out in those attempts to embarrass children that parents become so fond of around the time their kids reach the age of fourteen.

I was always unfazed by this particular tale, finding the anecdote to be rather brilliant. 'The Hot Willy Story', as it is now known, has become a family favourite, something I'm only too happy to recount in company, be it at parties, weddings or funerals.

It also lead to a realisation that my wife was the perfect woman for me.

The first time I told my then-girlfriend's parents about the time I stripped in Tesco to blow on my stiff penis – the charm offensive with the prospective in-laws had just gone into overdrive – they confessed that they had a similar story where Jennifer was concerned. She had apparently dropped her own skirt and pants down (accidentally, she *claims*) in the middle of the very same Tesco at almost exactly the same age. It was like we were meant to be; kindred spirits.

In fact, when I think of that occasion, I like to imagine that my future wife was just an aisle or two away that same day, baring her arse for the world to see at the same time I had my own naughty bits on display.

Finding someone with a common childhood memory has not proven to be an isolated incident; not by any means. In reminiscing about the nineteen eighties and nineties with family and friends, I've learned that many of the stories from my youth are echoed in the pasts of others, often by people who I didn't yet know back then.

My mate Andy, who I first befriended in my late teens, was able to recall very similar accounts of WWF-style wrestling in the school playground, grass stains and all, even though he went to school in Renfrewshire while I grew up in Ayrshire.

My brother-in-law Daryl, who I only met as an adult, grew up in the town next to mine and yet has tales of mistreating plant life just as I did. Downing beers and reminiscing about the nineties one night on a recent holiday, he told me how he and the other local boys once found a 'bouncy tree' – a sapling tree no more than a few feet high, not yet fully formed or upright, on which children could stand and bounce.

'But,' he added, 'there was always one wee dick who went too far and ended up snapping it'.

Excitedly, I roared with laughter about how I had experienced the exact same thing, just miles away and oblivious of my future kin.

Comparing childhood memories and games with new friends, we often discover differing regional names for common games. Every kid knows 'Chap Door Runaway', but some may know it simply as 'Chappy'. Daryl remembers playing what we called 'Granny', but says that his town knew the game as 'Gardens' – under either guise, it involved groups of wild kids running through consecutive gardens, vaulting fence after hedge after fence like an Olympic hurdler, much to the chagrin of elderly homeowners.

One of my granddad's favourite old lines is 'We went to different schools together', and that always springs to mind when a nostalgic chat wields common memories.

This book shouldn't read as the autobiography of a nobody. It should read as the autobiography of countless nobodies across the country. It should spark, I hope, happy memory after happy memory for the reader, either from identical experiences or just similar ones.

Some of the memories detailed within will seem like carbon copies for nineties' kids; no doubt everyone of that era remembers watching *Art Attack* after school, while surely every school class played 'Heads Down, Thumbs Up'.

Other tales may simply resonate with your inner child, or trigger long-forgotten, hilarious memories that are only slightly similar to mine. Perhaps you took your own streak through the pews of a church instead of the aisles of a supermarket. Maybe instead of driving a teacher to madness with a raft of whistling as my secondary school class did, yours pinged elastic bands around or staged a silent protest in order to drive Sir or Miss up the wall. While I cried at *My Girl*, perhaps it was *The Lion King* or *The NeverEnding Story* that moved you to tears.

Regardless, I hope that by looking back at my childhood together, we can share a few laughs about a decade I hold very close to my heart, and I can piece together where it all went wrong…

II: DIARY OF A MADMAN
'You made this for me? Aw, that's lovely... What is it?'

We children of the eighties and nineties shared experiences that no other generation can fully relate to.

We were the last kids to grow up without mobile phones an everyday sight; the only person we knew who had a mobile was Zack Morris on TV's *Saved By The Bell*, with his cell phone the size of a house brick. If the Bayside and Valley rivalry had ever come to anything, he could have killed someone with that thing. The iPhone can do many things, but you can't bludgeon someone to death with it.

Household computers were similarly scarce. External storage space was limited to floppy disk drives and their 3.44MB of data (not enough to hold even one modern MP3). Nowadays if you started chatting to someone about their three and a half inch floppy, you would probably just get arrested.

The World Wide Web hadn't even launched yet. When it did, we dialled-up using modems to get online, and incoming phone calls would kick us from the connection. Parents would hit the ceiling every time they picked up the house phone and heard that alien noise which meant someone was connected to the Internet.

As for looking at online porn, you could forget that unless you had a spare half hour of privacy in which to let the image load, line by line. Today's randy teenagers will never experience that fevered wait for a .JPEG to make it as far down as the tits.

Following the Rubik's Cube of the eighties, we had the Tamagotchi, Pogs and eventually the new yo-yo, with ball bearings for extra spin. Pocket money went on Panini stickers without fail.

Grunge broke, with Nirvana's now 23-year old *Nevermind* record.

Down south, Spurs' wonder-kid Gary Lineker (now 54 and as silver as Gandalf the Grey) topped the English Premiership goalscoring charts. Closer to home, a cheeky-faced Ally McCoist (now 52 and built like he has a training ball bag up his jacket) was banging in the goals.

Philip Schofield was no omnipresent silver fox but instead played second fiddle to a puppet, Gordon The Gopher.

Twenty five years ago, a little-known televisual newcomer called *The Simpsons* made its debut.

At the box office, films very much of their time such as *Ghost, Terminator 2: Judgement Day, The Addams Family* and *Honey, I Shrunk The Kids* hit it big.

John Major was the UK Prime Minister and George Bush was President of the USA, but as far as we were concerned, Sega and Nintendo ruled the world.

How times have changed.

Let us first dip our toe in the water of the nineteen nineties, scented as it is with Matey bubble bath from a pirate-shaped bottle, with a look at a diary I kept throughout 1994 and 1995.

My mum is even more reluctant to fully part with that decade than I am; her loft and several of her wardrobes are chock full of 'sentimental stuff' from the decade in which my sister Fiona and I grew up. On first glance, it's impossible to distinguish 'sentimental stuff' from 'dusty, useless shite', but the key difference is apparently that all of the former played some part in our childhoods.

Old boxes full of photographs, yellowing newspaper clippings and school report cards which throughout my academic career were peppered with telling comments like 'still needs to concentrate more', 'easily distracted and willing to distract others' and 'Graeme would get on a lot better if he listened to instruction instead of doing his own thing'.

Classic family photo albums full of hilarious baby photos - with plenty of nudity - often trotted out for family, friends and passing strangers in a misguided attempt to humiliate. The star of 'The Hot Willy Story' is, naturally, unfazed and just a little proud of these old Kodak prints.

Bin bags full of stuffed toys, a pram that hasn't been touched in almost thirty years, every item of artistic output no matter how awful; it's all there, somewhere. The loft floorboards are nearly at breaking point, our ceilings practically bowed under the weight of paper plates covered in paint, glue and macaroni.

Of course, my mum never sets foot up there and my dad has no time for that level of sentimentality, so none of it is ever touched. I cannot imagine any circumstance where the glitter-covered lump of modelling clay that I made one Christmas is ever going to reappear and serve a purpose. With storage space at a serious premium, I have to assume we are at the tipping point of my dad's sanity where the loft is concerned.

Other items of tat to be found in these haggard boxes (bearing now-defunct brand names) include pictures of Fiona with her old-school Deirdre Rachid glasses, letters home about MMR jags, hand-drawn comic strips and worst of all, the photo of a seven year old me meeting two of my heroes, Kilmarnock FC players Bobby Geddes and

Ally Mitchell, on their visit to our Primary 3 class.

How my mother ever thought the knitted, multi-coloured nightmare that was my jumper was a good look, I'll never know. Bizarrely, my older sister had a matching effort and together, we looked like the ends of a rainbow had shat all over us.

What should be one of the proudest memories of my school career is forever tainted by the horrendous, polychromatic monstrosity that was my knitwear. Behind the smiles of my footballing idols, I can't ever help but imagine them thinking 'Look at the nick of this wee diddy'. Thanks, Mum.

As snapshots of that era go, the highlight of the collection is undoubtedly the Primary 4 class journal of an eight year old me. Featured within are nights spent watching *The Generation Game*, shopping trips to spend pocket money on Mega Drive games and VHS entertainment such as the *Teenage Mutant Ninja Turtles*, Jim Carrey's early films and *Mighty Morphin Power Rangers*.

As the great Jasper Beardly would say, 'What a time to be alive'.

Other high points of the diary include tales of my infected elbow, my football coach Mr. Flannigan telling me I was 'getting better', the time I ate a lot of potatoes, and the day I got new slippers. I was a modern-day Anne Frank, channelling the spirit of Samuel Pepys.

22nd August 1994
On Saturday my nose was bleeding. It was the braces of my nose was sore. On Sunday I was racing Paul. I tripped and I had to put a plaster on my elbow. It was infected after I took the plaster off.

25th August 1994
I went to football training. Allan Mc Ginnes scored a goal. Mr flannigan said I was getting better.

29th August 1994

On Saturday I went round to my Grans house to see her extension. Its got a new carpet, new curtains and new chairs. It looks lovely.

5th September 1994

On Friday I went to the Viking Village but when I got there and it was closed. We had a look around and there was a stall where could win fish. I won a fish. It died on Saturday though. On Sunday my auntie, uncle and wee cousin and June and Eric came. There was a huge cookie for Eric.

12th September 1994

On Saturday I got new slippers with footballs on them. I also got a new pair of football boots. They are Gola.

16th September 1994

A few days ago I drew a picture and sent it in to a comic and tommorow I will see if I won the star prize. I can't wait. On Thursday I went to the family mass and I enjoyed it. There were a lot of folk there. I have got the cold and it is bugging me.

19th September 1994

On Saturday I went to my Gran's for my Great Grampa's birthday party. My Uncle George came to the birthday party as well. He bought us presents as well. He gave me a computer game and Fiona Aladdin on video. My Uncle George is a great uncle. My cold is still bugging me.

26th September 1994

Yesterday I was watching strongest man in the world. On Saturday I was at a football match. I scored a goal. I enjoyed it. My conservatory is started now it looks brilliant so far. I cant wait till it finished so I can get my new room.

3rd October 1994

On Sunday I could have went to My Auntie Laura, Uncle

Frank, and little Cousin Suzzane. But we weren't sure if the builders were coming. They didn't come. So my Mum, Dad, and Gran went to Makro while me and Fiona stayed with Grampa and Great Grampa. Me and Fiona played pretend restraunts and serving both Grampas.

10th October 1994

On Sunday I was playing with my friend Michael long he was on his bike and I was on his scooter. After that we played with our remote-controlled cars. Now my conservatory is nearly finished we can step on the floor of it. The glass is in and the steps are on.

17th October 1994

Yesterday we made up a new charity group. We named it CHA - Children Helping Animals. We voted for a committee - a president, a vice president, a secretary and a treasurer. At our first meeting our fundraisers decided on ten ways we could make money.

25th October 1994

On the first day of the holidays I was excited. I was going to York with my Gran and Grampa. I didn't enjoy the train journey it was bumpy. Our house was a Victorian cottage. We went all sorts of places like York Minster I enjoyed the railway museum best of all. I had a brilliant time.

31st October 1994

On Thursday it will be my birthday. Thomas, Paul, Louise, Amy, Adam, Grant, Michael, Mark, Fiona (and especially me) are coming to my party. And on Saturday I was playing in a football match. If we won we would get medals but we didn't win. In fact we lost 2-1. Paul scored our goal. After the match my Dad dried my hands with a towel because it was raining and my hands were like blocks of ice. When I got home I had a nice hot bath. After that I went for Grant. He invited me in to play his newest computer game sonic and knuckles. Half an hour later Fiona came over to tell me I had to go to the boring old shops in Irvine. We had to get a cooker ring. We took my Great Grampa with us. We met one of my neighbours. When we got back we watched The Generation Game. It was good.

7th November 1994

On Saturday my Mum asked me, Dad, and Fiona if we wanted to go to the fireworks display or stay and watch television. We all wanted to stay. We watched the Generation Game, Noel edmonds house party and family fortunes. On Sunday we went to the St. Enoch's Centre. I had £29.00 to spend. I bought a new computer game called Rocket knight adventures. When we got home we fed our dog and Fiona's fish then we went to the Ship Inn for our tea. When we got home we watched tele.

28th November 1994

My Mum knew a lady called Edith harrison. On Sunday Mrs mc Gough phoned to say she had died. And last night I prayed for her and her family. I feel sorry for her son and dog who lived with her.

On Saturday 26th November, Archbishop Thomas Winning became a Cardinal of the church. He is only the third Cardinal Scotland has ever had. At a special cermony in the Vatican, Cardinal Winning was presented with his red birreta by Pope John-Paul. Later he said "It was just heaven!"

5th December 1994

Today we will begin our preparation for christmas. The tree and decorations are up. In the afternoon we are going to sing carols for the senior citizens.

On Thursday I am going to the Chinese with Thomas Williams, his Mum and Dad. And sometime this week I will be moving into my new room.

12th December 1994

On Sunday I went for Grant but they were going to the Glens Car Park and they asked if I would like to go. I asked my mum if I would be aloud to go and Mum said "yes". After we had went invited me in to watch Turtles III. It was good fun.

19th December 1994
On Friday after the panto Mum thought we would be tired. So she went to the Azad video shop and hired Beethoven's 2nd. We took it back after the Christingle service on Sunday. But I saw a Power Rangers video. I've watched it already and it is very good.

9th January 1995
This year my new year resolutions will be. To play my computer for the limited time, tidy up my room and stop eating so many sweets. NOT!!!

30th January 1995
On Friday my Gran and Grampa took Fiona and I ten-pin bowling. At first I was doing really well. Then I started to lose, then finally I lost. After that we were supposed to go to Mc donalds but there was too much sleet so we went to Gran and Grampa's house for tea. When we got round the road I was sick.

6th February 1995
On Friday after school I started to write an 18 chapter story. Its a bit like fantastic mr fox but there's definately more chapters. It's called a fox's hole and its about a fox's family and a farmer's family who are both enemy's. The chapters I can't wait to do are called double trouble because the farmer's cousin comes and the other one is called the warehouse and weird things happen in that one.

13th February 1995
On Sunday my Aunt Sadie and Uncle Onie came to see us. At dinner time my Uncle Onie made a one pound bet. The bet was that I couldn't eat 10 potatoes in two minutes but I did.

23rd February 1995
On Tuesday Mrs McGough came round to discuss Children's Liturgy Group buisness. Matthew had come to cause there was nobody to look after him. He came round for 5 hours. We played the computer, we drew, we played hide the lion and we played football

and tennis. Then I had my dinner then went over for Grant.

27th February 1995
On Sunday Duncan Cameron came round to play. After a while he had to go for his dinner. Then I went up for my friend Michael Long. Fiona, Michael, Amy and Adam were all having bike races and I couldn't play because I can't go one. Amy and Adam wen't in and I was determined I would go one. So I got my bike out the garage and I tried to go it... but I couldn't. Then when Michael gave me a tip and I tryed it and I done it. Then me and Michael raced to the top of the estate and back down. I won. At the weekend Dad and Mum are taking me to kilburnie for a Mountain Bike.

6th March 1995
On Saturday I got a mountain bike. It's got my favourite colours dark blue, orange and grey. On Sunday my Dad put my mud guards on before we went to June and Eric's house. It was because I wanted a quick shot on my new bike. When we got to June and Eric's I played with his Skielekstracks.

13th March 1995
On Saturday my Uncle George came down. Fiona and I made up our own Radio station. We done it on Fionas Ghetto-blaster because you can record your voice on it if you have a spare tape and you are at least 50cm away from it. Our Radio Station is called GFTV news instead of GMTV and we have Mr Motormouth instead of Mr Motivator. Mr Motormouth is always bragging about his fishing trips. We pretended we were at Silverstone but we were really in my room and playing my Scalextric (and we were doing a bit of commentating) then we were at Rugby Park and the match was Kilmarnock vs Aberdeen but we were really in my bedroom playing Subuteo. The Final score was 5-5. After that we done an interview but it was only me putting on voices. We even recorded adverts off the tele.

20th March 1995
On Saturday I came out with rashe's all over my arms, back,

chest and my legs were covered in rashe's. Fiona and I made up a puppet show with our puppets. All the money raised we are going to send to SCIAF. On Sunday Michael and I went out on our bikes. then we had a game of football against his big brother Mark. The teams were me and Michael vs Mark. He was on his own cause he is 12 years old and me and Michael are only 8. The final score was 18-13 to me and Michael. It was a good game.

2nd May 1995

Yesterday I went to my auntie Jennys. We had to take Sam because we couldn't leave him in the house so long. There was a 2 hour drive there so we took a couple of breaks. My Dad played football with me at the first break then we stopped for a picnic Fiona and I played football then we continued to my auntie's. When we got there my Dad and Grampa took the dog a walk and I went too. I got to hold his lead (Phhew! he's STRONG)

15th May 1995

On Friday my Dad came home from work and said "My friend gave me a tape" his friend had said that it was suitable for us to watch. Later, I snaked into his room and to see what it was. it was The Mask. We watched it and thought it was good. We let Gran and Grampa have a lone of it.

30th May 1995

On Sunday I went away to the practise match for the 7-a-sides st Pauls are having. when I was tackled I stood up and looked like a Christmas tree. This is because we were playing on astro turf. On thursday I am going to a Davie Cooper Appeal match. The teams are tons of old football players who are now managers vs Rod Stewart and some of his friends who call themselves the L.A. Team.

12th June 1995

At the weekend I was playing football with my friends Mark, Adam and Michael. Then they had to go, so I went over for grant. I was playing his new computer game Theme Park. The idea of the game is, you are the manager of a theme park and you have to build tons of rides and stalls. At the end of the year you can sell your park and buy another one, so on.

19th June 1995

Yesterday my Dad cycled 26 miles. He cycled out the back way of Dalry, up to West Kilbride, then to the shore, through Ardrossan through Saltcoats then back again. That took him 20 miles. 5 minutes later he cycled 3 miles to Smithstone played rugby with me, played football with me, had 3 burgers then cycled back again.

III: KISS ME
'I'm no a V.L. - I got off with someone at ma gran's bit'.

In the nineties, it seemed that people the nation over were going to their granny's house after school and fighting off a throng of willing, easy suitors.

'You don't know her, she's no fae here'.

What's worse than the fact that our teenage years were spent dreaming up imaginary tonguing sessions with imaginary girls (and hot ones, at that), is that everyone believed it all.

Well, who were you to doubt that your trusted mate was a veritable Lothario with the girls who happened to live near his grandmother? Besides, the very fact you had no means of verifying it struck you as convenient; perhaps you could pass that story off as your own come the dreaded time someone challenged your V.L. ('Virgin Lips', or someone who's never had a snog) status.

Girls as objects of desire (rather than the enemy) was a concept that snuck up on me. Years of watching Zack Morris pursue Kelly Kapowski, Corey and Sean stuck in a love triangle with Topanga, Bart Simpson falling for Laura Powers, and the on-off drama between Ross and Rachel, eventually struck a chord with some primal instinct in my subconscious when I least expected it. Aged eleven, during Primary 7, I almost unwittingly stared to blaze – or fumble, really – my way through a trail of romances that were every bit awkward as young love should be.

My table group in our P7 class consisted of my best mate and 'brother from another mother', Thomas, Paul (the smartest and best-behaved of us all), Alistair (who would race with me to complete pages in our Maths books and cry under the desk whenever I beat him) and three girls, Kirsty, Isla and Stacey. By the end of the school year, Thomas and I in our individual romantic conquests had each worked our way round all three of our group's girls, with varying degrees of what I suppose could be loosely classed as success in those young days.

On one of our many unpermitted trips into the White Witch's forbidden garden – at the back of the massive, sinister-looking house which sat some hundred yards behind Thomas' – I had my first, lame romantic encounter.

All the usual tall tales and urban myths were told about this 'witch', the strange old woman whose huge, imposing manor sat alone atop a hill in the countryside, with an expansive garden like something out of *Sleeping Beauty*, surrounded by woods and full of crooked, dark trees and giant bushes in which small children could get lost.

This garden was one of our regular haunts. To survive a daring run through the White Witch's garden was a badge of pride for any local boy. Stories abounded as to what happened to anyone who got caught; all we knew was that they never reappeared.

All this mystery and intrigue was all well and good until the day that Thomas and I happened to see the White Witch in front of her house on one of our walks to the neighbouring Kittyshaw Farm.

Mrs. Yorke, as she introduced herself to us, turned out to be a lovely old lady. She was out pruning some flowers in the garden and was all too happy to chat pleasantly to the curious, scared little boys peering in at her giant, black gates.

In the weeks following, we did try to correct anyone telling tales of Dalry's White Witch – we had seen her with our own eyes, spoke to her even, and she was just a wee granny out tending to her flowers – but kids were having none of it, and the legend of the White Witch lived on.

Personally, all thoughts of terror where the White Witch was concerned left my body that day when, as we stood nervously talking to her, her dopey black labrador started dragging its hind legs and arse across the driveway.

The romantic encounter in question, in which I first tried my luck with a member of the opposite sex, happened one day that we snuck into Mrs. Yorke's garden with Kirsty Roberts in tow. Taking a girl in for a daring jaunt was seen, by us, as adding a real touch of adventure. Once inside and safely ensconced in a clearing in some bushes, we fed her some scare story about Mrs. Yorke…or the White Witch…and her dangerous pack of rabid dogs, and how they had once chased us.

The reality – that we had watched her idiot lab cheerily wipe his arse on her driveway, while we laughed uncontrollably with the safety of a locked gate between us – was a closely guarded secret shared only by Thomas and I.

Stories embellished and tension suitably ramped up, with visions of wild slobbering dogs ready to burst out at any moment, Thomas left us alone for a while as we had earlier agreed whilst pre-planning this little tryst – by way of announcing he had to run home for a shit, of all things – and so off he popped. Or pooped, more accurately.

At that, Kirsty and I had a fumble in the shrubbery. As I recall, it went something like this: I touched her knee, rubbed my hand up her thigh, she smiled back at me, and I moved in to kiss her cheek.

Afterwards, we sat chatting inanely as kids do; here, the childhood equivalent of kicking back under the covers and having a cigarette once the action had simmered down.

Thomas reappeared, there was an awkward pause, and the three of us returned to our playful ways, climbing in gardens we shouldn't, running out in front of cars and no doubt kicking a ball.

Later, with Kirsty gone, Thomas asked how things had gone and I reported back in earnest. No V.L-busting girls at Gran's or otherwise made-up romance where Thomas was concerned; together, we were helping each other to navigate the awkward trials and tribulations of young love, and to do that successfully we both knew we had to be honest about our experiences. If I realised that getting a quick rub of a girl's thigh and a peck on the cheek didn't amount to much, then I had to soundboard ideas with my best mate to get a sense of what I could improve upon the next time I found myself horny in an old woman's bush…

Anyway, who better to discuss it with than Thomas, the only other guy I knew who had had a fling of his own with Kirsty? Back in Primary 6, during French lessons and while sat next to me at a table of four, he and Kirsty had had it off under their Adidas tracksuit trousers.

As Tommy relayed it to me later that day in the playground, he had reached under the desk and touched her leg, at which Kirsty invited him in for further rubbing by opening the poppers on her 'three-stripes'. Luckily, Thomas was also wearing poppers – trackie bottoms with buttons running up the length of the three stripes, all the rage in the nineties but mysteriously disappeared from today's sportswear market – and the touching of bare leg could be reciprocated.

Incredible. It may have taken him a week longer than I to learn 'My name is Thomas, I live in Dalry', but with eroticism like that going on, you could keep France and its complicated language full of male desks and female tables.

In comparison to my touch of the thigh and peck on the cheek, their romance was a real thrill ride of sex and emotion. I was Billy Zane's Cal Hockley in that year's romantic smash *Titanic*, officially her current suitor but by no means her most exciting; Thomas was Leo DiCaprio, drawing open her buttons like one of his French girls.

For my next flirtation with the opposite sex, I asked Isla Hart if she fancied 'going out' as we waited one day for the morning bell and she said yes; perhaps Kirsty had given good reviews of a date with Graeme Johnston, I thought proudly.

What Isla probably didn't know is that this was a marriage of convenience. Yes, she was good-looking, but more importantly she sat next to me at our class table.

Annoyingly, she never seemed to wear easy-access sportswear, instead favouring plain black trousers, but in life, nothing worth doing is easy.

Later that morning, probably approaching some sort of anniversary by the short-lived terms of childhood romance, I made my move. As Mr. Howden nattered on about something to which I paid no mind – it was some years later, with my dad's help, that I mastered long division, so it may well have been that – my legs and Isla's became entwined. I wrapped my right leg over her left and started sliding it up and down in an awkward rub. She responded by bringing her own right leg into the mix, rubbing it along mine. I began to wonder why my side of the desk was in danger of being lifted by my crotch.

The buzz of it all was short-lived, as that afternoon I was left – not for the last time - scratching my head as to what exactly it is that women want; Isla split up with me at lunch, a friend acting as the bearer of bad news, as was always the girls' style. Even now, having been together with my wife for twelve years and married for five, I still dread the day that her best mate asks to stop a game of football for a quiet word with me.

This love business was confusing. Both my best friend and I had rubbed a girl's leg under the school desk, all concerned parties had seemingly enjoyed it all, and no one had anything to show for it apart from a few burst buttons and an embarrassing term spent sitting next to our now-exes.

Well, I wouldn't make the same mistake with my next love interest: she was 'the one'. Stacey O'Neill, I finally came to realise, was the girl I should have been chasing all along.

Of course, the fact that she was the only girl left at our table group for me to try and woo was irrelevant. That wasn't the reason for my interest. She was smart, beautiful, and shared her surname with the news reporter from my favourite show, *Teenage Mutant Ninja Turtles*. Seriously, what more could an innocent young guy ask for?

I came to realise that I loved Stacey as we worked together on a 'Mary, Queen of Scots' project, strangely enough. For our display, Mrs. Tailor wanted a life-sized drawing of old Mary on the wall and as two of the most artistic, Stacey and I were paired up and sent out to the gym hall to get to work. As we lay there on the gymnasium floor, happily colouring in the queen's dress and mindlessly chatting, sparks began to fly. It really sums up just how clueless we all were in this game of love that one of her appealing qualities was, apparently, that she could colour within the lines.

I asked her out at break, via my best friend Thomas and her best friend Emma, who only days previously had got together. The whole thing was perfect, not one but two matches made in Heaven.

In fact, so pleased were we with our intertwined love lives that I remember Thomas and I, on more than one occasion, playing games where we would wrestle off imaginary dangers to our girls. With him bouncing around on his bed and I on his brother Daniel's, we would punch, drop kick and wrestle with completely invisible thugs – thin air, basically - who were trying to hassle our imagined, not-there girlfriends. That's how cool we were. Is it any wonder we were making our way round the school desks?

Stacey and I's relationship flourished. I bought her a

teddy for Valentine's, my mum driving me to the house to drop it off as Valentine's Day fell on a weekend that year. I spent afternoons at her 'bit', joking with her mum and playing with her wee brother, all in an effort to impress. We went for walks in the park.

All that was missing was a kiss. Thomas and Emma were stalling on the same front. How could either of us be considered real boyfriend material if we weren't prepared to man up and lock lips with our respective partners? Time was ticking, and our girls wouldn't wait forever.

One day, walking up the dirt track to the Kittyshaw Farm, we devised an ingenious plan. We would bring them up here, on a pointless walk to a random farm as courters the world over so often would, then make our move.

Just then, we found some six-inch nails by the side of the road and as boys tend to do with discarded crap discovered underfoot, gave them undue significance. These nails, we decided, would show us where to pounce. We placed them in a mound of grass next to a gate and agreed that these markers would spell the end of our status as 'virgin lips'.

Our passing the nails would be the cue for Thomas to drop some cock-and-bull story about needing to turn back. Hopefully it wouldn't involve pooing this time.

I wanted to go on, I would announce to Stacey. Our foursome split up, we would be alone with our girls and all the romance of the surrounding cow fields. That, we had decided, would make for the perfect first kiss.

Of course, come the time, both of us royally shat it, and as the four us walked further and further past some stupid nails at an arbitrary point which Stacey and Emma knew nothing about, the horrible realisation of our cowardice sunk in. Neither of us had had the courage to enact the plan and so we walked on dumbly to the farm, both girls probably wondering where the fuck we were going.

The farmer appeared then, and told us we couldn't be

up here. We about-turned sheepishly, and lead the confused girls back past those same bloody nails, each of us silently cursing the markers and our failure to act.

I was to get a second bite at the cherry some days later, as Stacey and I enjoyed another of our strolls around Dalry's public park, with her friend Emma in tow. Best friend or no, she wasn't welcome in my book – a gooseberry who could only serve to cramp my style.

Out of nowhere, Stacey took my hand in hers. Electricity ran the length of my arm; a girl's hand, my hand, together! This was the kind of mad thing you read about in books or jealously witnessed in awe during movies. Yet here she was, a girl, and our hands interlocked. I could barely contain myself.

'Why haven't you kissed me yet?' she asked suddenly.

'No reason', I said, angrily picturing those useless nails in that bloody mound of grass, as I had done so many times since.

'Kiss me now', she said.

Emma looked on, expectantly, no doubt hoping beyond hope that she was about to witness her friend's coming of age.

'I… can't', I said, my brain wrestling with my tongue and furiously wondering why those words had just left my mouth.

'Why not? Kiss me!'

'I… can't. You've got lipstick on!'

What the hell? Who was saying these words? These crazy statements sounded, frankly, like they were leaving my mouth. Why?!

'So?' she asked, indignantly.

'My mum says I've not to kiss girls'.

Shat it. Again. Completely and utterly shat it, like an incontinence sufferer with the runs. Nailgate all over again.

That is literally the worst thing I've ever said, I thought to myself, with no small amount of self-loathing.

'Your mum?' they both laughed. 'Don't be silly. Just

kiss me!'

'No', I said, more serious this time. 'My mum says I've not to kiss girls'.

It was bad enough the first time! Why on earth had I said it again, and so sternly? It sounded ten times more stupid the second time round. I was making this out to be like something in an American teen movie – I was the nervous young cheerleader, Stacey was the arrogant high school quarterback trying to force herself upon me in the front seat of the car he'd parked down some dark 'lover's lane'.

A girl, finally wanting to kiss me – a boy who had spent almost every moment of the previous few months daydreaming about kissing girls, specifically this one. On a plate and I turned it down like I was full up, when in fact I hadn't even eaten yet.

Here we were, Stacey and Emma excited at the prospect and me, hopeless, scared, pitiful. Onlookers expecting a firework display and me pointlessly standing there, fizzling out like a pathetic, burned-out sparkler plopped in a bucket of water.

Needless to say, Stacey and I didn't last much longer. I never caught wind of how that episode played out in the gossip mill of the playground, but I wager not well.

Many suffered similarly humiliating failures in their younger days. My mate Gav grew up in Pollok, and remembers one of his first romantic encounters involving his then love interest, a friend and the friend's girlfriend of the time. They ended up in a quiet area of a park, the two couples with all of their clothes off, trying (but failing) to work out the biology of how they could have sex. Naked, they rubbed their bodies against each other, his arse in the air going like a fiddler's elbow, nothing of note happening... Was sex all it was cracked up to be?

My friend Matt has even worse memories of that period in his life. 'Mad', as we call him – he resembles Alfred E. Neuman of *Mad* magazine – relayed this story to us at a music festival some years ago, as we sat having banter round the campsite fire.

The conversation was 'Best ever gig' and Matt dropped Alice Cooper on us. Wrong.

We debated the four best Metallica albums. To everyone else, this was simply ordering *Kill 'Em All*, *Ride The Lightning*, *Master of Puppets* and *...And Justice For All* (which, incidentally, is *MOP* first, then *AJFA*, *RTL* and *KEA*).

Not Matt. He lists *Metallica*, *Load* and *Reload* in his top four. Horrific.

Then the conversation turns to 'At what age did you lose your virginity?', and while most of the twenty-strong group of campers bore us with stories of being late teens or early twenties and getting five minutes of missionary, Matt hits us with a bombshell.

'I was early teens'.

'What?!' we all cry.

'We were in the woods'.

Yes. Everyone sits forward.

I pipe up with the obvious question on all our minds: 'Were you drinking some cider from a three litre bottle?'

'We were drinking some cider from a three litre bottle.'

This tale was suddenly taking a turn for the fantastic.

'Me and my mate were there with two girls. They both wanted a shag, so I took one and did her against a tree'.

Protection?

'Err, no. So, we finished up and I thought that was that. But then she tells me she wants go back to her place for more'.

So what happened?!

'I told her it was my bedtime and that I had to go home. So I went home'.

Amazing. I can't help but wonder how long he waited for his second shag and how painfully he regretted, every day, choosing 'bedtime' over her offer of more.

Epilogue to the story - his mate kindly obliged her in

Matt's stead.

While Gav was struggling to stick his bits in a girl's, and Mad Matt was squeezing in just one bout of sex before curfew, I spent weeks and months ruing my missed opportunity with Stacey.

Some time later, as Alistair and I were playing with his wee brother Andrew at the river that ran through the public park, we saw the girl who was still the love of my life.

It never occurred to me that this river was just a short walk from the very scene of my doomed romance, my devastating failure to lock lips with my girl; not even when Stacey appeared at the opposite side of the water, walking her King Charles Spaniel with Emma and their friend Deborah.

Clearly I wasn't quite ready for romance; my mum had no need to be buying a fancy hat any time soon. After a short-lived, happy wave between the six of us, one of us boys decided to start tormenting the girls. Soon, all three of us were throwing rocks at them, for no apparent reason.

I was in grave trouble later that night when it transpired that a rock I had thrown had hit the spaniel in the eye. Stacey's mum had taken it to the vet and ended up with a three-figure bill. Relationships frayed.

So here I was. Turning down the first kiss I was ever offered by the only girl I wanted to kiss, ruining our blossoming relationship and some weeks later, throwing stones at her and her friends, accidentally smashing her beloved dog in the eye. Smooth.

There seemed no end to this journey in sight.

Surrounded by beautiful Irish countryside, we rolled over horizon after horizon to be met with further miles of Class Z road. Were we doomed to drive along this glorified BMX track forever more? Just then, the car provided a solution of its own, by breaking down.

The Vectra spluttered a terminal wheeze and rolled to a stop.

'Fuck', cursed my mum.

I was aghast. This was a real collector's item; my mum swearing. Not only that, but uttering the f-word no less.

It drove home the severity of the situation, like seeing a bomb disposal expert fleeing a crime scene. If Mum was swearing, times really were bad.

She was on the money, though: no car, no sign of life, no phone signal and no means of contacting anyone who could help.

We set off on foot, looking for a house and some means of rescue. I had to hope we would find one soon. My stomach was starting to churn like a boat in a storm. Something was wrong.

I needed a restroom. Somewhere, anywhere. Any port in a storm…

IV: WICKED GAME
'If you come in one more time, that's you in for the night!'

One of the greatest pleasures in life must surely be poring through the Argos catalogue, circling any toys that catch the eye for an impending birthday or Christmas. Many things can take the mind back to those halcyon days of Argos-scouring and the gifts that went with it.

The smell of burning rubber can remind me of the overuse of Scalectrix.

A drenching in the rain is not always unpleasant; often it transports me to the time when Super Soakers were all the rage and the protest cry was 'Ma maw says I'm no allowed tae get wet!'

Something as simple as a cardboard box throws up memories of building a lair for my Teenage Mutant Ninja Turtles, using boxes discarded from the local supermarket, with straws fashioned into ladders. Turtles were actually so popular one year that it took my gran bringing them back from a holiday to Italy for me to get my grubby little mitts on them; the figures were impossible to find in British stores for a time as there wasn't enough stock to meet demand. The warning not to aim at other people was routinely ignored as I used the TMNT pizza-firing truck to shoot hard orange discs at my sister's face whenever the notion took me.

Subbuteo was a boyhood staple. We once borrowed my uncle's video camera and filmed a game for TV broadcast, adding in Archie Macpherson style commentary to boot.

Anything collectable was assumed to be our path from rags to riches, with toy sets the cornerstone of many children's get-rich-quick schemes. The world still awaits its first millionaire made rich thanks to a full complement of Beanie Babies, though not for the want of trying.

Many shelves were decorated then with a line of Corinthian football figures. Creepy-eyed Furbies lay uselessly in the corner of rooms across the UK. Gogo's Crazy Bones, while insanely collectable, were the bane of teachers everywhere – the cause of arguments, prone to theft and the reason why many pupils were driven to distraction.

Pencil toppers were also popular in the classroom, with kids eating inordinate amounts of cereal in order to force mums to buy more boxes with more toppers.

Whoever first hit upon that idea of putting free toys in cereal boxes is a marketing genius. We would munch through Ricicles box after Ricicles box if it meant the potential for the new figure in a set of toys.

Some of these collectables were stupidly popular: so many of my childhood friends remember the glow-in-the-dark Casper stickers given away with cereal in conjunction with the release of the 1995 movie. Just recently when clearing out a mate's old family home we came across a wardrobe still bedecked in decals of Stretch, Fatso and Stinkie.

In reminiscing about these great days, common memories are often found. Upon finding an old set of bed sheets recently, I took a photo and shared it online. Within twenty four hours, I had found more than a dozen mates or strangers who had the same duvet set of Sonic The Hedgehog racing across a starry night sky. We each swapped pictures: not one of the twenty-something year old grown-ups had brought themselves to throw the old sheets out, so they were dug out of cupboards, gleefully put on for the first time in decades, photographed and uploaded to the internet.

Houses full of Casper stickers and Sonic bedsheets. Garages full of bicycles with Frosties lights adorning their spokes.

Some of the best toys were dirt cheap or free. Bikes would boast not only those Frosties lights, but empty plastic bottles squished and stuck into the spokes: the effect was a piercing, rumbling noise that made your bike sound like a revving car.

Toys could safely be launched from high surfaces with nothing more than an empty carrier bag for a parachute. 'Is it a bird? Is it a plane? No, it's Action Man tied to a Safeway bag!'

Other common toys of the time included Boglins, Hungry Hungry Hippos, Mousetrap, Stretch Armstrong, remote controlled cars (with the connecting cable which frustratingly meant you always had to be within three feet of the car), and Barbie dolls, who would be stripped naked and made to engage in sex acts with male figures by little brothers everywhere.

Boys' collections of dolls would begin and end with WWF wrestling figures, with all their accoutrements (match ring, ladders, championship belts, clubs and other weapons). Some of the characters would perform moves – clotheslines, karate kicks or punches – at the touch of a button.

In any group of lads, one guy always wanted to script every move and slam of a twenty minute epic match to be acted out by the figures in question, while the rest were just happy to take two figures and bash them together wildly; most WWF figures had had the paint scraped from their chest long ago.

More than any other toy or collectable, there was one thing boys really wanted their mum to buy them on every trip to the shop: Panini football stickers.

Nowadays, I would be hard pushed to tell you more than three or four players from most of the teams in the Scottish top flight. Then, I could name just about every player in the league, down to second-choice Dunfermline full backs and Partick Thistle youth players just breaking through: if they were in that year's Scottish football sticker album, I had studied their face countless times on one of my many flicks through the book.

Come August, chores got done without any nagging and pocket money got spent on one thing and one thing alone: sticker packets. The buzz never lessened, not even after tearing open a new packet for the hundredth time: that fevered wait to see which stickers the pack contained, what doublers you were landed with this time ('Stevie Crawford again?!'), whether or not you would finally nab that ever-elusive Celtic badge, the Wonka's golden ticket of Scottish football stickers.

There was just something so satisfying about sealing another player into your precious tome, no matter how obscure or crap the player: whether it was Dragoje Lekovic of Kilmarnock, Dougie Arnott of Motherwell or Ben Honeyman of Dundee United, adding another sticker to the collection always felt immense.

While most packets were procured with pocket money, others were obtained via the aforementioned hassling of parents. A small fortune must have been spent on stickers. In fact, every season with each new album, there always seemed to be that one time that your mum just broke down and surrendered to splurging on a dozen packets, even a box of packets, in the desperate hope of some nag-free peace.

It was like Christmas come early. Nothing felt better than being handed a massive pile of new packets. The wait to get home to your album was chronic.

This was an occasion, a time to completely clear your schedule, sit down alone to properly enjoy the tearing open of every packet, slowly going through each set and examining each individual sticker.

Every sticker would be placed with great precision, to ensure it fitted perfectly within the appropriate rectangle. There was something very therapeutic about the whole process.

Of course, no album was completed with purchases alone: an absolutely essential part of collecting the stickers was trading with your mates. For many boys, some of their strongest childhood memories involve sitting down in the school playground, snapping back the elastic band from their pile of doublers and bedding in for a good trading session.

'Got, got, need...'

Collectors had so many different rules where trading was concerned. Clearly a shiny could be traded for a shiny, but was also worth at least two players. Anyone trying to negotiate a straight shiny for player swap was laughed off. Some stickers made only half a picture, with the completed album image two stickers wide, so these were often deemed to be worth more, too. Certain players also became valuable in trading circles – Alan Archibald stickers might be ten a penny one season, while Andy McLaren 'in action' could be rarer than hen's teeth (although inevitably, like buses, three would eventually come along at once).

Finishing an album produced a great sense of pride. The temptation to stick such an achievement on the current C.V. is huge ('Once completed the Panini World Cup 1998 Sticker Album'.) Eventually there would be just one sticker left to find: anyone who had it to trade could bag themselves a real windfall, the massive pile of doublers you would no longer have any need for, all traded for the sake of that one final sticker.

When we weren't smashing our wrestlers together or fighting over doublers, we were usually to be found outside getting up to mischief.

Full days could be spent with games of Slapsies, Last Hit, thumb wars, mud fights, Wally and climbing trees.

Thinking back on the very best childhood games practically lifts me from the modern day and drops me back in the early nineteen nineties. I still hanker for the day the old gang gets back together for one more game of…

Kiss, Cuddle, Torture

Players would separate into boys and girls. Boys would huddle together and assign the letters A, B and C to the three choices of kiss, cuddle or torture. For instance, it might be agreed that torture was A, cuddle B and kiss C.

Once letters had been assigned, the girls would be given a few seconds in which to escape, before the boys each made a mad, unabashed dash for the girl they fancied most.

Upon catching the girl of their dreams, boys would scream 'Kiss, cuddle or torture?!'

The girl in question would shout one of the three possible letters in reply and would then get kissed, cuddled or tortured, depending on what action had been assigned to their chosen letter.

That's how it worked in theory. However, the game came to an abrupt end when the girls eventually compared notes and realised that regardless of which letter they picked, hot girls inevitably got slipped the tongue while troglodytes got a kick up the arse or a dead arm for their trouble.

Hidey

Another name for 'Hide n Seek', a good game of Hidey could go some way to helping ditch the reprobate who no one wanted to hang out with. Some poor, unloved sods were kept hiding for hours, wondering why their pals still hadn't uncovered their bang-average hiding spot.

Another variant of this game was 'Hidey Tig', where before they could 'tag' a mate, whoever was 'It' had the added challenge of finding one of their four hidden pals.

As we had the run of the town in those days, players could be stashed away just about anywhere within a two mile radius. Games would last for hours, as some lonely soul ran around the streets desperately looking in bushes and up trees for their mates.

For their part, the hiders would usually lie down in a brilliant spot among some tall grass, oblivious of any surrounding dog shit, then immediately start willing the seeker to find them, having only just realised that they really needed a pish.

Heads Down, Thumbs Up

A classroom treasure, 'Heads Down, Thumbs Up' saw the teacher pick three kids to stand in front of the class. The rest of the class would put their heads on the desk, eyes closed, with their arms outstretched and thumbs up.

The three chosen kids would then go round the class silently, each gently pushing down the thumbs of one pupil before stealthily returning to the front of the class.

The aim of the game was that everyone in the class then opened their eyes and the pupils who had had their thumbs tapped took it in turns to guess who had touched them. A correct guess meant you swapped places with whoever had tapped you and thus got a shot of sneaking around.

The success rate of guesses was stupidly high, due to the fact that everyone kept their head bowed and eyes closed only until the person had tapped their thumbs and about-turned, taking a peek just in time to see the shoes of the person who had put their thumbs down.

The game wasn't so much about correct guesses as it was about being able to recognise shoes. Still, pupils adored it in spite of the copious amounts of cheating that went on.

I was reminded of the game recently upon hearing a song by DJ Isaac that goes 'Face down, ass up, that's the way we like to fuck!'

'Face down, ass up'? God knows what school he went to, but their classroom games must have been horrific.

Den building

At least one day of every summer holiday would be spent building a den.

After the discovery of a perfect spot, a gang of local kids would club together to oversee the project. Jobs would be assigned, resources found, and a safe, private haven where the gang could chill out during their holidays was crafted.

Our best ever den featured different rooms – with areas cordoned off using traffic cones formerly deployed at roadworks – a couch that we had found waiting to be uplifted at the side of a pavement, a smashed up telly that had been dumped nearby, and an old rug, the origin of which was never quite established. Some poor pensioner is probably still wondering whatever happened to the throw that she left out to dry on her washing line.

'Right guys, we're it – don't tell anyone who's not in the gang'.

Inevitably – usually within twenty four hours – some motormouth blabbed and the gang would return to find their den in ruins.

Bogies

An amazing rite of passage for any young lad, 'Bogies' were a great thrill that I shared with my mate Peter. Thankfully, it didn't involve snot *.

Bogey is a slang term for go-karts. We spent hours,

* Peter did actually have a bogey stool - quite literally a stool in his bedroom onto which he would wipe his bogies, the underside a veritable graveyard of old, dried boogers - but that's irrelevant. So is the fact that he once confessed to having a crush on Taylor of boyband Hanson after spying them on my sister's copy of that week's *Smash Hits*, before I broke the news to him that none of the *MMMbop* singers were female. That's completely irrelevant. Sorry, Pete.

days even, building and modifying a go-kart from wood, old toys, bits of rope, pram wheels and anything else we could find. Think Bart's soapbox racer, Li'l Lightnin', in the *Saturdays of Thunder* episode.

We must have been the only homemade go-kart owners in Scotland who had a wing mirror on their beloved bogey. As soon as I saw the circular mirror lying by the side of the road, presumably having come off a motorbike, I thought how perfect it would be for those moments when we had to reverse the kart into a tight parking space, or as a precursor to signaling and manoeuvring.

The great irony of adding such a safety-oriented accessory is that while riding our bogey we defied all health and safety, common sense and rules of the road.

Peter lived on St Margaret's Avenue, which for several hundred yards sits on a massive slope, with streets coming off at either side. Starting at the top of the hill for momentum, Peter and I would fly across these adjoining streets at the T junctions where they met St Margaret's, making for a death-defying run that was over in seconds; terminally so, had we ever hit an unseen vehicle.

With no means to check for cars coming out of junctions, no way to warn them that we were about to shoot across the road, unseen, milliseconds before they made their turn and most importantly, no effective brake, the whole thing was, on reflection, one of the most dangerous things I ever did as a child.

On one of the back pram wheels we had screwed on an old piece of wood that could be turned until it lay against the wheel, making a rudimentary brake that would create enough friction at slow speeds to ease the kart to a halt. In the event of flying downhill into a junction to meet an oncoming car, the brake would have been about as useful as a fart in a spacesuit.

In a similar vein, I once reminisced to my wife, Jennifer, on how the waterfall in the glen next to my house would freeze over in extreme winter weather. As kids, groups of us would head out onto the top of the waterfall, thirty foot or so high, and slide around on the freshly frozen surface.

Catching flies and with eyes like fried eggs, Jen barked: 'And what if you had fallen through the ice?!'

I sat quietly for some seconds, genuinely chilled as I processed the very thought, and admitted: 'We, err, never thought about that'.

In hindsight, some benevolent force may have been watching over me as a child. However I survived, all I know is that we had a lot of fun dicing with death.

Only now do I confess such escapades to my mum. Needless to say, she doesn't see the funny side.

Jobbies

This is a game that some may know as 'Bogies', which confusingly does not involve go-karts. Or stools. Not of the wooden sort, anyway.

It involves increasingly loud shouts of the word 'Jobbies', 'Bogies', or indeed anything else which may cause profound embarrassment for accompanying adults in public spaces.

Starting as a whisper and with participants taking turns, the challenge is to see how loud someone is prepared to go to be crowned the final, loudest participant and therefore overall champion.

For the boldest players, the ideal setting is the classroom. Starting off as just a whisper, the utterings of 'Jobbies' are at first funny only to those in close proximity. The louder the cry becomes, the more surrounding pupils join in with the laughter, until eventually the whole class is aware of the game.

Once the teacher has registered her first 'Jobby' shout, it takes true daring to attempt another, louder shout and live to tell the tale. Many a champion savours their victory only until being ordered down to the year head's office.

Much of the joy of a public game of 'Jobbies' stems from the fact that most if not all of your surrounding audience are unfamiliar with the game and therefore have no earthly idea why a group of kids are shouting about bowel movements.

As an adult, I overheard a game of 'Jobbies' being played on a recent trip with family and friends to the Kelvingrove Art Gallery in Glasgow. Almost without thinking, I joined in.

Hearing my cry repeated and improved, I was willing to go one better, until the realisation hit me that I was now an adult and in doing so, I would be denying a child the unrivalled joy that comes with a winning 'Jobbies!' shout.

I bit my tongue, did not shout 'Jobbies' for a second time, and let that little kid bask in the glory of his victory. Proof, surely, that I have matured as a person.

Urban exploration

Urban exploration is a phenomenon that is becoming increasingly popular as a cost-free form of adventure. The hobby largely involves trespassing in unusual, dilapidated or closed-off areas where members of the public are not supposed to frequent; abandoned factories, old buildings, former underground tube stations and so on.

I became fascinated with reading tales from such places – derelict hospitals, old wartime shelters – and with the whole culture of sneaking in to these dusty old buildings maintaining the urban explorer's motto, 'Take only photographs, leave only footprints'.

It was only as I read more and more on the subject that I eventually realised that I had once been an urban explorer myself – having spent much of my childhood trespassing on sites and properties that were out of bounds to the public, as kids do the world over, breaking laws and putting myself in no end of danger.

There was the vacant house near my pal Tommy's house, with rumours of ghosts that haunted the scene of a supposed murder. We snuck into the overgrown garden one day, peeked in the dusty windows and even tried a back door, before hearing a noise, scarpering and ending up peeking out from some jaggy bushes we had leapt into without thought, as a smug cat strolled past and gave us a condescending look.

There was a ramshackle cabin in the local park which we used to force our way into via the skylight, usually as a place to set fires or do a pish.

There was also the old building behind the local Chinese restaurant. We snuck in one lazy Sunday afternoon after pulling back a piece of wooden boarding. Inside, we discovered an abandoned warehouse, covered in dirt, dust and damp, falling to pieces, with a toilet out of which grew a massive ivy-like plant. We snuck up what was left of the rotting wooden staircase, discovered a drinking den upstairs – the entire floor covered in empty beer cans – kicked around enough that we disturbed some rats, and snuck out again with no one but the vermin any the wiser.

British Bulldogs

British Bulldogs was as much a staple of the playground as Bench Ball was of the gym hall, and was undoubtedly a daily topic of conversation and debate within the teacher's staff room.

One player would be chosen as the 'bulldog', while the others would stand in either one of the two 'home' zones at either end of the play area. In each round, the aim was to get from your current home zone and across to the other without being tagged by the bulldog.

Anyone who was tagged became a bulldog too, and so the winner was the last untagged person left in the game.

The reason that trouble arose – and it became such a matter of consternation for the poor teaching staff – was that any bulldog trying to tag a fellow player had to grab hold and cling to their subject for the duration of the chant

'British bulldog! One, two, three!'

Thus, a game of British Bulldogs looked every inch like a men's rugby training session. Bulldogs would fling themselves at the opposition, rugby tackling players to the ground and wrapping their arms around the knees of their intended target until they had finished their manic shout.

This was fine if the game was being played on grass, but all too often it involved pinning small kids against brick walls whilst shouting in their face, or doing a lunging takedown on concrete.

We all loved it, but eventually the teachers got sick fed up of cuts, bruises, broken bones and angry letters from parents, and put a stop to it. British Bulldogs was banned.

Eventually, a game that was identical in all but name, called Octopus, also got banned. As did Seaweed. And Shark. And British Sharks. And British Wall. And Bulldog Wall. And Bulldog Rush. And Bull. And any other variant under which we tried to disguise the opportunity to rugby tackle each other into walls.

Kerby

Without question, Kerby is the game that most of my Scottish friends most fondly remember. It doesn't matter what sort of upbringing you had, what street you lived in, where your town was or who your friends were: if you grew up in Scotland, you played Kerby.

As an aficionado of the game who last played it just a year or so ago on holiday, I love discussing the sport (let's officially start recognising it for what it is) with mates who grew up in other towns and cities. Local variations and rules inevitably come out in discussion, but the basic rules are always the same.

Kerby, like so many games in our childhood, was yet another pastime that was often interrupted by cars. Bloody motorists and their constant need to get from point A to B, always interfering with the innocent fun of children. Beasts!

KERBY

Standing on opposite pavements, you and your mate would take turns to throw a ball at the other's kerb. If you hit the kerb with the first bounce of the ball, this was counted as a point. The winner was the first to amass ten points.

A successful hit permitted the chance to step onto the road to the point exactly halfway between the two pavements. From there, you could aim at the kerb for up to five consecutive hits, each time gaining a point, or until you missed.

A missed shot made for one of the most terrifying experiences in a child's life. From that dreadful moment, it was an anxious race between you and your mate: you to get back as quickly as possible to your pavement, unscathed, and your mate to grab the ball and throw it at you. A successful strike of your body as you made your way back to the pavement was a point to them, and the opportunity to stand at the halfway point for five throws.

Different means of showboating added a bit of bravado: flair could be added with a backwards, blind throw over the head, by throwing the ball over the roof of a passing car, or by stepping backwards onto the lawn of a neighbour's garden and doing an extra-long throw. A successful combination of all three would see your name officially recorded in the town's history books as a proper local legend.

Truly, the sport of champions. Every couple of years I await the news that it has been added to the Olympic or Commonwealth programme, and am eternally disappointed. Forget China, America, Australia: Britain would bring home a clean sweep of golds in Olympic Kerby.

V: HOME SICK HOME
'Sorry, I'm too old for that now. I am going into secondary school you know…'

My first look at the diary I kept in Primary 4 - republished in all its splendour in Chapter 2 - in more than twenty years transported me back to one of the greatest times of my life, to memories I had almost forgotten.

Looking at this veritable time capsule afresh, for the first time as an adult, my views on many of the events detailed within have shifted significantly since I first wrote it, aged seven.

For instance, I have come to the conclusion, with hindsight, that I was a boring wee git as a child.

Experiencing wonderful little snippets of every pupil's childhood, any good teacher goes home at night feeling that their life has been enriched by that day's most touching moments in which they shared with his or her children.

I'm sure that learning of 'The Cooker Ring Shopping Trip' was one such moment for Mrs. Pearson. She must have been riveted: like the cliffhanger at the end of an episode of *24*, the end of that story surely left her devastated that there wasn't more detail for her to immediately feast upon.

What shops did we visit and where did we eventually get the cooker ring?! What size and make was it?! How much did the ring cost?!

Providing such scant detail, leaving so many tantalising mysteries dangling for the reader to contemplate, shows all the hallmarks of a classic young writer at the peak of his powers.

There was certainly some enthralling stuff detailed within that diary: notes on my gran's decorating, a cold that was mentioned in several entries, and a night in front of the television.

How disappointed the teacher must have been when, on 7th November 1994, I started the paragraph with the possibility of a fireworks display, only for it to nosedive into detail of an evening instead spent watching *Noel's House Party* and other Saturday night telly fare.

My then-version of events concerning our trip to York differs greatly from my recollections as an adult. There's so much wrong with the entry detailing the holiday we took with my grandparents that I scarcely know where to start.

I claimed not to enjoy the train journey because 'it was bumpy'.

Actually, I ended up in tears on the journey to York not because of anything as ridiculous as the bumpiness of our transport, but because it was my first time away from home and the rapidly-diminishing sight of my mum stood waving on the station platform broke my little heart.

Secondly, it's baffling that I would claim to enjoy 'the railway museum best of all' when the undoubted highlight of the trip was seeing *The Lion King* in the cinema. A fucking railway museum over *The Lion King*? I think not, seven year old Graeme.

I also neglected to mention that this was the trip on which my gran and I had the only argument I can recall us ever having, over the fact that I spent all of my pocket money on day one (on a magnetic Sonic The Hedgehog pinball machine), then cried on day two for my gran to give me more.

In fact, looking back, my overall memory of York is basically that I was a dick.

My realisation that I was a bit of an arsehole is compounded by the entry of the 31st October 1994, where I state: 'After that I went for Grant. He invited me in to play his newest computer game sonic and knuckles'.

While that in itself may not seem too bad, what is shaming is the memory that I was never normally invited into his house as claimed: what would actually happen was that I would brazenly invite myself in.

I would regularly chap his door to be greeted by his mum:

'Is Grant coming out to play?'

'I'm afraid not', was often the answer.

'Well can I come in then?'

If any of my son's pals ever have the bare-faced cheek to hit out with such a presumptuous suggestion, they'll be getting sent from the doorstep with a boot up the arse.

Instead, I was heralded into Grant's bedroom thanks to his lovely mum and her saint-like patience.

Grant and I made for such an ill-fitting friendship that I'm amazed how often we would spend time together. We were as different as chalk and cheese.

He was the geeky, indoors sort, very prim and proper, who owned his own chemistry set.

I was the scruffy, usually mucky, outdoors kind, regularly to be found inviting myself into people's homes. I once nearly set fire to our house in a misguided attempt to melt chocolate onto toast under the grill. Letting me loose with a chemistry set was never even a consideration.

Personality, humour, loyalty; none of these things were high on the list of attributes I looked for in a friend. Instead, living in the same street as me and owning a vast collection of Mega Drive games were far more important. I would often play Sega games for the first time at Grant's

(*Sonic & Knuckles*, *Theme Park*, *Worms*, *Cannon Fodder*) then head home to bend my mum's ear about buying them for me.

'Try before you buy' was my motto.

In return for a good shot of his new computer games, he had someone he could call a friend, whether he wanted one or not.

Now with a father's perspective on events, it seems I would either give my dad too much credit or not enough. If I wasn't gushing about the fact that my dad had cycled more than twenty miles before stopping to play sport with me – deferentially adding such as detail as the fact that he 'had 3 burgers then cycled back again', painting him as some sort of real-life Desperate Dan – then I was completely failing to recognise the work that he put in to teaching me how to ride my own bike.

According to the entry of 27th February 1995, 'I tried to go it… but I couldn't. Then when Michael gave me a tip and I tryed it and I done it.'

My poor dad gets nary a mention, despite putting in hours and hours of bike-riding training with me over several frustrating, aborted sessions spanning months. All credit goes to Michael for that one tip that I 'tryed' then 'done'. I wonder what it was: 'Keep pedalling'?

Speaking of not giving folk due credit, I can't help but feel I had a case to answer from the estate of Roald Dahl. It seems I was working on an eighteen chapter story that was 'a bit like fantastic mr fox but there's definitely more chapters.'

To be fair, based on my description of it from February 1995, it's 'a bit like fantastic mr fox' in that it has a different name but is otherwise exactly the same as *Fantastic Mr. Fox* – even, despite my holding it aloft as a key difference, down to an identical number of chapters.

Likewise, an investigation by the Scottish charity regulator must be imminent. I expect there may be some tough questions to answer about the practices of CHA

(Children Helping Animals).

As far as I recall, no charitable work whatsoever was carried out by the organisation, helping animals or otherwise. More likely, we spent an afternoon raising a few quid from gullible neighbours and spent the proceeds on lemon Sparkles and Mini Milks.

Looking back through it all, I also realise I wasn't nearly as smart as I thought I was.

One flick through a diary which includes stories of me playing with 'Skielekstracks', coming out in 'rashe's', the time I 'snaked' into my dad's room to check out our VHS of *The Mask* and being 'aloud' to do something confirms that I wasn't the child genius I once believed myself to be.

That same dusty old box of sentimental crap in which I discovered the diary boasts other, equally illuminating, tell-tale souvenirs from my primary school career:

- A piece of work from the last days of Primary 7 in which I list my ambitions as becoming a footballer and 'spare time cartoonist', getting married on the centre spot of Rugby Park, playing for Killie, keeping in touch with friends, meeting the Spice Girls and, most bizarrely, 'to be in a Lyons Golden Syrup Advert'.

- A letter I wrote, in order to help my mum and gran with their newly-opened genealogy research company, which reads: *'Dear Mr Paton we are nearly did all your history. From graeme Johnston (marys son)'*

Its inclusion in the box indicates that for some strange reason, my mum never posted it to Mr. Paton.

- A postcard written to the local bishop regarding the upcoming Confirmation service of pupils in our P7 class. Clearly the point of the correspondence was that we formally request he attend our service to confirm us into the faith, but predictably I treated this as an excuse to go off on a tangent about football.

'To Bishop Taylor
Please come to my Confirmation on Tuesday 26th May to confirm me. I am a mad keen Killie fan and don't miss any games. I am a loyal Paul Wright fan. He plays for Killie. I hope you do not like Harald Brattbakk as Celtic beat us 4-0 once, and he got all of them. (BOO)
Best Wishes
Graeme James Johnston'

It was approved, signed and returned without comment. Apparently Bishop Taylor wasn't up for a bit of football banter. I began to suspect that he did in fact like Harald Brattbakk, so shot him dirty looks throughout the service.

- A Christmas card to my mum, on the inside of which is scrawled:
'To Mary Johnston
wishing you good luck for your diet and also Merry Christmas
Love Graeme xx'

- And a letter to my long-suffering mother that was presumably sent on a Valentine's Day mired in misbehaviour:
'Roses are red, violets are blue
I'm sorry for the bother I've caused you.
Mum,
I'm sorry for the selfish and bad behaviour I've caused you lately. I know that you and dad have been in a terrible state lately because of me. I didn't mean to make you feel like that. I still love you and I always will.
Yours lovingly,
Graeme Johnston'

One of my most treasured finds from the box is the scrapbook that I compiled at the end of my last term of primary school education. Each school year is summarised in ridiculously economical descriptions. For instance, a whole year of my life can apparently be boiled down to the fact that I helped run a hot dog stall which was 'quite successful'.

MEMORIES OF ST PAUL'S
BY *Graeme Johnston*
June 1998

PRIMARY 1
I remember my first day at school when Miss Baker had to show me to the toilets and I got locked in. I remember feeling proud when we got measured and I got to wear a sticker saying "TALLEST".

PRIMARY 2
My clearest memory of primary 2 was sitting reading 'Meg's Castle' when my best friend at the time, Stephen, told me he was leaving for Aberdeen. I cried for ages. And when Patrice and Kevin came in to watch us, we got measured and I was taller than Patrice.

PRIMARY 3
I remember Thomas Williams kissed Stacey behind the blackboard! I made my First Communion that year.

PRIMARY 4
I remember a student teacher, Miss Murray, took us to the library to do Mapstart and Alistair dropped his pencil to look at her legs. I remember writing a bad word in my jotter and I got caught.

PRIMARY 5
We had a hot dog stall at the fun day. It was quite successful.

PRIMARY 6
T.S.B. Cup! For the first time, St. Paul's Football 'club' won a trophy, and I scored a goal in the tournament. Just before the school year started I met Paul Wright. He is more than a hero to me. But that was not the end. He scored in the cup final to win us the game.

PRIMARY 7
During this year, I achieved my life ambition. At a tournament at Rugby Park, I captained my team, and scored from the half way line. Primary 7 went to York this year. It was quite good. I have enjoyed my life at St. Paul's, and I will enjoy my life even more when I play for Killie.

Primary school done and dusted, 'TALLEST' stickers and blackboard kisses and all, I had given a fairly accurate, if brief, summary of each year. Looking at the entry for Primary 7, I can only assume there had been an injunction placed on recent events which prevented me from so much as mentioning the biggest and most memorable incident of all.

It - that which thou shalt not speaketh of - had happened just days prior...

It was the last few weeks of our time in primary: it was very nearly time to move up to the 'big school', St Mark's Academy.

The journey from Primary 7 to S1 is one of the biggest transitions of any child's life. The act of going on to secondary is scary, not a little exciting and a time when kids tell themselves they have made it to the promised land of adulthood.

With still a healthy dose of naiveté, innocence and immaturity deep down, S1s desperately hope to command the respect that comes with the tag of 'young adult' - striving for maturity with a new dress sense, adult language and the eschewing, outwardly, of anything deemed childish.

For many kids, there comes one day in particular when they decide that they are ready to shake off childhood, embrace adolescence and make that fateful, giant step into their teens and everything it brings.

That came for us one morning towards the end of our

P7 tenure at St. Paul's. The buzz was out: a teacher was visiting from the secondary school to take our class for the afternoon. Mrs. Tailor, our beloved teacher in our last year of primary education, was handing over the reins to Mrs. McLeod, a teacher of English at our soon-to-be place of education, St Mark's Academy. This would be a monumental day we would remember for the rest of our lives.

Unfortunately, it would pass into infamy for all the wrong reasons. After a particularly good or bad day, it's common for teachers to head home and unload on their families, sharing their highs or lows with significant others. Mrs. McLeod's husband must still rue the day she agreed to take our class for a couple of hours. What a chewing that man's ears must have suffered.

The day started innocuously enough for all concerned. Word went round at playtime: Mrs. Tailor had commented in passing to some of the girls that we could look forward to a visit from one of the secondary school's English teachers later that day.

Some furious discussion on the subject of secondary school duly ensued. Many of us had big brothers or sisters. We had heard the scare stories of playground fights, vicious birthday 'dumps' and hordes of kids walking the playground smoking cigarettes or worse. Some had thrilling, half-remembered tales from older friends of first kisses or even lost virginities.

There was all manner of talk about the responsibility afforded to children deemed more mature for having made the step to secondary, the rule that teachers had to be addressed as 'Sir' or 'Miss' and the fact that we would now be taught in six equal blocks, or 'periods', by six different teachers a day. It was all fascinating.

For my part, I contributed a titbit of information my neighbour Adam, one year older than I, had shared with me: that in first year science, there was a topic in the biology curriculum officially called 'Section Six' that covered every young boy's favourite subject. However, pupils at Garnock Academy, where Adam attended, had taken to giving it the hilarious yet appropriate new name of 'Section SEX'.

Needless to say, if this nickname wasn't already in use at St Mark's, I wanted to be known as the witty card who brought it to the table (I was, of course, too late).

After playtime and the last part of the school day to be taught by Mrs. Tailor, we spent our lunch break playing 'Polio'.

Each classroom had a raised square ledge outside its door, roughly two feet by two feet, with a small black railing. 'Polio' involved players running between two of these ledges, some twenty feet apart, each considered a den. The aim was to avoid whoever had been deemed 'it' or 'het' as they tried to grab you in the middleground. Anyone tagged then became another chaser.

Upon making it to the other side, players had to touch the black railing to signify entry to the den area - only after grabbing this black pole were you safe for another round, hence the bizarre name 'Polio'. It had nothing to do with the virus that the DTaP/IPV/Hib vaccine protects against, which was probably just as well.

Humour was always to be derived from making a show of travelling between these two poles – passing between the two points comically slowly while the chaser was otherwise occupied pursuing a particularly elusive player.

On one such occasion, I aped an old woman crossing a road with difficulty, garnering laughs by loudly proclaiming 'Make way for elderly pedestrians' as I cautiously hobbled across with my imaginary walking stick.

It became tradition for players to do this whenever the chance arose. As soon as the chaser was far enough away, some comic would break out this hysterical elderly pedestrian routine and we would all fall into fits of laughter.

I became quite precious about people getting laughs

with my material, worried that not everyone playing knew that I had originally started this huge joke. Whenever it happened, I would make a point of obnoxiously reminding anyone who would listen that I was the first to hit out with this brilliant bit of observation comedy. Eventually, I sapped any humour still remaining in the bit by endlessly boring on about how people had to pay homage to the inventor of this routine if they were going to use it.

I was such a knobhead. (Some would argue I still am.)

Our game of 'Polio' finished, the bell ringing out to signify the end of lunchtime, we headed back to our classroom. En route, I triple-checked that everyone knew that I was in fact the person who had come up with that fantastic 'Make way for elderly pedestrians' shtick. It seemed everyone did. Good.

There were fourteen Primary 7 pupils that year, and each did a double-take upon entering the classroom: Mrs. Tailor was nowhere to be seen. Here stood a stranger in her place. Not only was Mrs. McLeod - presumably, this pleasant-looking teacher who was greeting us as we walked back to our seats - going to teach our class this afternoon, but Mrs. Tailor was not even going to be there with her.

That fact really added to our fever pitch. Our days of primary education felt truly behind us; while we knew normality would be restored tomorrow, for today we had only one teacher, and that was a secondary teacher. That made us, in essence, secondary pupils. This was massive.

Mrs. McLeod introduced herself, asked that we quickly state our names and a bit about ourselves (making a joke of the fact that she would have forgotten us all by the start of next term) and gave us a brief overview of what life at the academy would be like.

From her point of view, this must have seemed set up to be a nice little afternoon, as she looked round at more than a dozen polite kids held in rapture while she spoke of what lay ahead.

She really could have had no clue as to the horrendous

rivers of bodily fluids that were about to attack her senses and ultimately fill the rest of her working day.

Soon, she put us to work on a writing exercise. Probably, this was no different to many such activities we had done before throughout our primary careers, but we embraced our first high school task with relish.

Tongue at the side of my mouth, pencil enthusiastically scorching across the page, I paused to think on what I would say next in an effort to impress our new teacher. I glanced around my table group. There were four desks pushed against each other, arranged in a tight rectangle. Immediately to my right sat Isla Hart. To our left, at a ninety degree angle to us, were Paul Callaghan and Stacey O'Neill. On our right was Alistair Sullivan. Facing us from the opposite side of the tables were Kirsty Roberts and my best mate, Thomas Williams.

As I scanned the room in my daydream, looking for inspiration from my muse, I caught Tommy's eye as he looked up to do the same. We excitedly raised our eyebrows with a wide grin passing between us, as if to acknowledge what wonderful men we had become. Before dropping our gaze, Thomas silently gestured to offer me a Locket from the packet he was working his way through.

At that, I remembered that he had told me earlier he had a sore throat and cold. He had almost not made it to school, but his mum had encouraged him to go. I declined his offer, and thought nothing more of it, except for noticing disinterestedly that he had almost finished a full tube of the throat-soothing sweets.

Everyone present in St Paul's Primary 7 class that day – especially Thomas and Mrs. McLeod – now knows that on the side of a packet of Lockets is printed the following warning:

'Overdose of menthol may cause severe stomach upset, being sick, giddiness, shaking, and drowsiness'.

We did not know that then.

Mrs. McLeod walked from table to table, paying a

friendly visit to each individual pupil. She leaned over our shoulders, quietly asked what we were writing about, and swapped some affable small talk in a bid to get to know us all a bit better.

As I looked down from Thomas and back at my work, she moseyed across to the other set of desks where Jason, Gemma and a few others were working scrupulously on their big assignments.

In an instant, my essay suddenly ceased to exist or matter. It was aborted in one vile flash, as the paper I was writing on disappeared without warning under a deluge of vomit, never to be given another moment's thought.

My brain was playing catch-up. In those first disgusting, foul-smelling moments, I made about as much sense of the situation as a dog reading James Joyce's *Ulysses*.

Slowly, the horror of it all filled my consciousness just as the pungent stench commandeered my sense of smell. Like the scene in *The Exorcist* frequently voted one of the scariest moments in cinema history, Thomas had projectile vomited across the desk, the contents of his stomach violently landing on my lap without invitation.

Suddenly and without doubt, I had a new number one on my own personal list of 'The Most Disgusting Things That Have Ever Happened To Me'.

That would be a very short-lived first. It was about to be replaced.

In a state of shock, I slowly brought my arms into my field of vision and turned them over with what must have seemed fascination, as though I was seeing them for the first time. I looked past my dripping appendages and surveyed the wreckage.

Around our desks, every child had anguish etched upon their traumatised faces. Thomas especially looked horrified at it all, frozen there with his mouth hanging open and drips of carrots falling away from his bottom lip.

I looked away from him to Kirsty Roberts, recalling as I did so that she had an uneasy relationship with vomit:

she had once told me that she could not see or smell vomit without being sick.

No sooner had that thought entered my mind than it was demonstrated in glorious technicolour. Kirsty's vomit spewed forth with a tortured howl, her worst fears realised as she lost whatever personal battle she had been fighting to hold back this involuntary voiding of her insides.

Kirsty's launched lunch mixed with Tommy's bodily fluids. Every inch of the desks was now covered – the chunky liquid ran off the sides like a Niagara Falls nightmare.

Those of us not having an out of stomach experience were at least having an out of body experience. From that initial state of confusion, I felt myself snap straight back into the room with that revolting second blast. I was able to properly take stock.

Here I was, sat in a place so full of happy memories, my school uniform soaked through in chunder.

Since Thomas' initial eruption, not even ten seconds had passed when that second stomach bomb went off. Proper consciousness regained, I caught sight of Mrs. McLeod's face as she stood like the rest of us, speechless, aghast at what was happening and powerless to do anything about it.

My attention was rapidly snapped elsewhere, as there was another scream for 'HUGHIE!'

Three separate rivers of barf came together, forming one overflowing lake of yellow, porridge-like waste before running off the desks.

While Thomas and Kirsty had both heaved in the same direction, across the table to Isla and I, Alistair's vomit came from our right, meeting the current flow of puke from a right angle. This had the effect of changing the current somewhat, pushing some of the offending liquid downstream, towards Paul and Stacey's end of the table.

Children all around the room were starting to cry.

The puke, now one great, flowing liquid, ran off all

four sides of our adjoined desks. In fact, some of it had begun to drip through the gaps in the tables, and I became aware of some splattering on my shoes and the schoolbag I kept underneath.

Mrs. McLeod finally tried to take action. She began yelling at us: 'WHERE ARE THE SPONGES?! WHERE ARE THE MOPS?! WHERE ARE THE CLOTHS?!'

'UNDER THE SINK!' we yelled back, because no one in a room with that much vomit could do anything but scream.

I'm still not sure to this day how she thought a couple of jay cloths were going to improve the situation any.

As our dumbfounded teacher scrambled around in the cupboard under the sink looking for cleaning utensils and trying to stave off her own shell shock, we pupils simply sat wordlessly staring, distraught, at the atrocity before us.

Just twenty seconds earlier, as we happily wrote our essays, no one could have possibly imagined the malodorous Hell that had lain in store for us.

Mrs. McLeod appeared with a little bucket and brush in her hand, like she was ready to pick up a shite by the clean end.

She stood holding them, looking at the table and the situation that she wanted to somehow contain, trying to figure out a way that two plus two could make bananas.

What must have been going through her head at that point, as she fought to regain control of a class full of strange children she had met only half an hour ago and who had just filled the room with their regurgitated playpieces? The sheer devastation in the room was magnificent.

Of course, every great performance has an encore.

This had all become too much for me. The ordeal of being covered in the filth of three other children is hard to explain to anyone who has never suffered that fate. Your senses suffer an overload, as your sight, smell, hearing and even sense of taste try to come to terms with the worst experience they have ever been asked to handle.

I could bear it no longer. My queasiness rising past boiling point, I liquidated my own assets all over the spew-covered desks. I turned my guts inside out, made my own crust-less pizza, shouted at my shoes, gave food offerings to the Gods, curled and hurled, and sneezed chunks.

We were even, Thomas and I. As we sat there sobbing miserably, tears running down our faces and into our vomit-filled mouths, we were even. He had thrown his sick up in my direction, before I had returned the favour and sent him an offering of my own.

It was now nigh on impossible to find a corner of the room that was not drowning underneath the produce of our four stomachs. That previous number one on my 'Most Disgusting Things That Have Ever Happened To Me' list had slipped into a distant fourth within the space of less than thirty seconds.

The fourth ejection of soup-like disgrace was the last straw for Mrs. McLeod, who had handled everything we had thrown at her valiantly enough to that point. She turned on her heel and with a blood-curdling shriek, loped out of the room, never to be seen in St. Paul's again.

It was some time until help arrived. Until then, we sat in near-silence, the only sound in the air the drip-drip-drip of the dinnerlady's 'Meal of the Day' running off our tables.

If this was what secondary school was like, they could count me out.

Some months later, the P7 class pupils almost fully recovered from the dreadful things we had witnessed that day, I was sat in a classroom under Mrs. McLeod's tutelage once more. Our first year at St Mark's Academy was a couple of weeks old and in our first period of this particular day, we found ourselves in English class.

Teachers, I decided, would surely not mind if I shared their worst secrets with a class full of new pupils.

This was an opinion I still held in fifth year at the age of fifteen: Mr. Thorburn, our new Computing teacher, must have thought he had safely left the embarrassment of his infamous cycling story in the past, at his previous school.

Unfortunately for him, my older sister Fiona had moved to Kilbrenning Academy for her final year, and so had been part of the class who eagerly learned one morning: 'Mr. Thorburn won't be in today, as he's accidentally cycled into a workman's trench…'

On his second day in front of a St Mark's class, I stuck my hand up and cheerfully asked Mr. Thorburn about the time he had ridden his bike into a massive hole in the road. When he seemed reticent to recite details, I did a fairly good job of giving a blow-by-blow account. He seemed displeased, but the class at large loved it.

So, naturally, it seemed a good idea in the early weeks of English education to boldly ask Mrs. McLeod if she remembered 'that day you came to our primary class, and we were all sick everywhere, and you ran out of the room screaming?' – like that was something you could possibly forget.

The rest of the class sat in rapture, enthralled as I recounted with a huge grin the time Thomas had eaten too many Lockets, before we filled the class with rivers of sick.

Mrs. McLeod sat wordlessly, staring off into the middle-distance amidst the howls of laughter and groans of revulsion, still unable to fully comprehend the awful things she had witnessed that day, like Principal Skinner lost in a Vietnam flashback.

Some years later at one break-time, my friend Chris told our group of mates that he had just seen Mrs. McLeod sneaking whisky into her coffee mug between periods. I don't know if that's true, but if she really was drinking, I had an inkling as to what had driven her to it.

The producer of Lockets really ought to make that warning on the side of the packet a good bit bigger.

VI: IDIOT BOX

*'What have I told you about sitting so close?
Your eyes will go square!'*

Every generation has convinced itself that popular culture was never better than when they were growing up; that modern toss couldn't hold a candle to the shows and sounds of their era. However, when children of the eighties and nineties assert as much, they are in fact totally correct.

How could Justin Bieber and the like ever compare to an age that gave us *Knightmare*, *Cool Runnings*, The Smashing Pumpkins and *Earthworm Jim*?

TV, film, music and video games. We were absolutely blessed where these corners of pop culture were concerned, growing up in an unparalleled golden age of entertainment.

With the small screen, kids could sit enthralled for hours enjoying such classics as *Trapdoor*, *Biker Mice From Mars*, *Dinosaurs*. In cinemas, audiences flocked to watch *Jurassic Park*, *Men In Black*, *Aladdin*. Blur went toe-to-toe with Oasis while across the water, Michael Jackson battled Nirvana in the Billboard charts. Gaming came into the home with two of the biggest-selling consoles of all time,

Super Mario's SNES and Sonic the Hedgehog's Sega Mega Drive, finding their way under Christmas trees year in, year out.

TV was king. Kids' television was never better, the VHS was at the peak of its popularity, games consoles plugged into the antenna slot via an RF cable and MTV was the big new thing in music entertainment. The television was our generation's iPad - the go-to device for all of the technological entertainment you could possibly want.

Following the school bell, it was a race to get home and fire the gogglebox on, ready to sit enthralled with whatever line-up of brilliance CITV had in store for us that day.

I was so eager to get parked in front of the television before channel three surrendered itself over to a nation of kids for the afternoon that I once ran through straight from my bath without even bothering to dry, to ensure I didn't miss a minute of the action.

My lips started turning blue right around the time that Scooby Doo's gang whipped the mask off that week's 'ghost', and I was marched back to get towelled down and stop shivering.

Dave Benson Phillips was telling kids to *Get Your Own Back*. Zack and Slater were fighting for the attentions of Kelly Kapowski (sigh) in the unbeatable *Saved By The Bell*. Sonic was running around trying desperately to get his hands on chili dogs (somewhat inexplicably) in *Adventures of Sonic the Hedgehog*.

We also had a litany of shite, British-made television to choose from including such drivel as *My Demon Headmaster*, *Grange Hill*, *Byker Grove* and *The Queen's Nose*, the show that inspired a nation of kids to optimistically rub fifty pence pieces out of vain hope.

Bernard's Watch was surely the worst of the home-grown dross, a series about a little boy with a magic watch that could freeze time who wasted his magic powers helping grannies and saving cats stuck in trees rather than successfully robbing banks or perving on women's changing rooms.

Other classic shows included *Gamesmaster*, *Pinky And The Brain* and *Funny Bones*.

After an afternoon of unrivalled class, things would finish on a high with the daily Sky One double-bill of *The Simpsons*, back in the days when it seemed *Bart the Daredevil* – the episode where Homer fails miserably to jump Springfield Gorge on Bart's skateboard – was on daily rotation.

Weeks would then be rounded off beautifully on a Friday by that week's episode of *Fun House*.

'It's wacky! It's fun! It's crazy! It's outrageous!
Fun House, a whole lot of fun, prizes to be won!
It's the real crazy show where anything goes!
Fun House, it's a quiz, it's a race, a real wacky place!
Use your body and your brain if you wanna play the game!'

Presented by children's television favourite Pat Sharp, with the help of cheerleading twins Melanie and Martina Grant (names permanently embedded in the minds of nineties' kids, despite being televisual non-entities since), the show pitted two teams of kids against each other in a series of contests.

Each week, the losing team would be taken out back and shot in front of their parents, the studio audience and the millions of kids watching at home.

(In reality, the worst that participating children actually had to fear was a gunging, that great staple of nineties' British television.)

Contestants would start with a couple of messy games in which a good gunge would never be too far away, followed by a go-kart race. Memorably, the race would end with the affable Sharp counting the tokens each team had collected during their laps on the track, dropping them into the respective coloured buckets.

The winners would finish the show off with a hunt through the studio set for prize tokens, with the ultimate aim of finding the Power Prize. This would vary week to week, but was usually something like a trip to a theme park.

However, with the Power Prize token often missed, contestants would win a truckload of crap instead: prizes were things like calculators, personal stereos, tracksuits, watches, walkie talkies, backpacks, fishing sets, and other obsolete junk that would now get overlooked at a car boot sale. Back then, we gawked with jealousy at the winning kids going home with handfuls of colourful tat.

Art Attack was the big one as far as after-school programming went, though. Neil Buchanan's ability to take useless shite like finished loo roll, polystyrene cups and bits of sticky tape and turn them into lovely ornaments or colourful decorations was the envy of every schoolchild in Britain.

Each segment would conclude with a stone bust puppet called The Head recapping the steps then showing viewers his own attempt at producing the creation in question, which usually ended with disastrous and hilarious results. This would have been funny if not for the sad fact that your own attempt usually looked no different.

While Buchanan could use everyday household junk to make cracking pencil tubs, Christmas tree decorations and scrapbooks, unhappy kids nationwide were left with bits of crepe paper Pritt Sticked to their fingers, strands of wool through their hair and only an empty toilet roll pointlessly sellotaped to a paper plate to show for it.

In a further effort to rub salt in the wounds, the presenter would then head outdoors for the show's most anticipated moment, the 'big Art Attack'. This involved him going out to some exciting location then creating a massive image – so big that the final result was shot in a bird's eye perspective from considerable height – using items and materials. For example, he once made a depiction of a skier on some snow-covered hills.

I was eternally disappointed that the segment never

concluded by revealing a large-scale cock and balls. If someone gave me a bunch of old jumpers and bed sheets and asked me to create a picture of anything I liked, to be seen from far and wide, a penis is still the first thing I would think to make. It's the first thing any guy would think to make.

How could Neil resist? Any money says he did it at least once and the editor bottled leaving it in.

You can certainly be sure that that sort of mischief did happen within the confines of our television studios: the cast and crew of kids' TV show *Rainbow* once filmed an adult-themed episode in which the three much-loved puppets (Zippy, George and Bungle) discussed wanking. Originally shot only for the eyes of Thames TV staff, the episode leaked onto the internet and is now widely available online, traumatising anyone who fondly remembers watching the otherwise innocent series.

Few things can sour your happy childhood TV memories quite like seeing George talk about pulling his twanger or genial host Geoffrey telling viewers to bounce their balls.

The episode opens with Zippy peeling a banana, counting to himself: 'One skin... Two skin... Three skin... Four...' - before George mercifully interrupts him.

But just when you think it surely won't get any lewder than a hint of innuendo, the puppets move onto the whereabouts of the other characters.

'Zippy, where's Bungle?' George asks.

'Oh, I think Geoffrey's trying to get him up'.

Cut to a door, from behind which we hear Bungle.

'Oh! I can't get it in, Geoffrey!'

'Well, you managed it last night, Bungle'.

'Yes, I know. Well let's try it the other way around...'

BOOM! Right in the childhood!

While you're still reeling from that, the two emerge (revealing that they had, in fact, been discussing some toys, which they have in their hands) and introduce the episode's topic: playing. 'With each other'.

There are memorable quotes such as:

'Are we going to play with our friends' balls today?'

'Rod and Roger could get their instruments out; and Jane's got two lovely maracas'.

'I was banging away all last night with Rod and Roger!'

'It doesn't matter what size your twanger is'.

And 'I've only got a tiny twanger, but it works well. I like to play with it'.

YouTube's adult version of *Rainbow* typifies how the World Wide Web has pulled back the curtain on fondly-remembered classics from days gone by, decimating many cherished memories.

One widely-accepted tenet of the internet is known as 'Rule 34', which states: 'If it exists, there is porn of it. No exceptions'.

I mentioned this to friends recently, who seemed utterly aghast at my claim that I could find them porno versions of ANY of their favourite childhood cartoons.

'No chance'.

'I promise you. Anything. All I have to do is search for it coupled with the term "Rule 34". Try me'.

We started with something wholesome, a cartoon so big and decent and well-loved that it stood to reason that no human being could possibly have sullied it by adding a cock:

'Thomas The Tank Engine'.

It was more a statement than a question, not so much a challenge as an indignant assertion that I was wrong, and this show would prove as much.

Wide-eyed laughter swept the room as, together, we browsed the 'net and found images of Thomas with juicy big tits, mounting The Fat Controller, and getting fucked by a variety of other trains. Yet more hilarity as we discovered a video called 'Thomas The Wank Engine', chock full of sex, swearing, violence, self-harm and suicide.

But behind the laughter, beyond the smiles and the tears of hilarity, I could see the pain that each of them was hiding; could see the moment that the inner child of each of my friends took a punch to the gut, witnessing the favourite choo-choo train of their youth cheerily giving James a blowie.

The next attempt to prove me wrong was with obscurity: Tom had let us down quicker than his own knickers, the little blue whore, so this time it was the turn of my pal Andy and the admittedly very good shout of *Sharkey & George*.

A French-Canadian cartoon from the late 1980s about the 'crime busters of the sea' - two fish private detectives - never since repeated on television: that had to be obscure enough that it hadn't been defaced, just by dint of the fact that the internet pornographers were too busy drawing vaginas on household names like Thomas and Mickey Mouse and Homer Simpson, right?

Wrong. The depraved picture that accompanied the porno *Sharky & George* sent another surge of shock, awe and explosive mirth around the room, before the caption 'Hymen busters of the sea' caused one guy to choke on his beer and another to leave the room to catch his breath.

'WHAT THE FUCK IS WRONG WITH THE INTERNET?!'

We changed tack, from 'too big' and 'too obscure' to 'too innocent', hoping beyond hope that no one had sleazed-up everyone's favourite honey-loving bear. Nothing can rape your childhood quite as horrifically as seeing Piglet tossing off Winnie the Pooh.

'Postman Pat?!' someone cried, desperation and trauma resonating in his high-pitched voice.

'Oh, there certainly will be', I insisted. 'Called "Postman Scat" or something equally chilling. And it'll no doubt have Pat taking Jess up the arse', I added, typing into Google as I spoke. 'Oh my god, Jess is giant... and Pat's got him bent over the Royal Mail van! WHY?'

Back in the day, the thought that such horrid, graphic imagery would be available at the mere click of a button would have completely astounded us. Then, it was a military operation to see so much as a pair of droopy tits like fried eggs hanging on a nail and a bush that wouldn't have looked out of place atop the napper of Jimi Hendrix.

Launching in 1997 – at almost exactly the right time in my adolescent period – Channel 5 brought pornography into the homes of randy young boys in a way previously thought impossible.

Every weekend, 5 would show a different bawdy and trashy British comedy from the seventies – tat such as *Up Pompeii*, *Confessions of a Window Cleaner*, *Adventures of a Taxi Driver*, *The Amorous Milkman* – and young lads across the country would consult with parents as to their plans for the evening, slink off to bed for an 'early night' and spend a night under the duvet covers, one hand on the telly remote (ready for a quick change of channel if needed) and the other hand otherwise occupied.

The World Wide Web would one day bring screeds and screeds of porn catering for all tastes into the home, but back then, all we had to keep us ticking over was paper-thin comedy plots, the all-too-occasional bit of boob, and fannies like beards.

It was a more innocent time, long before any sick individual had even thought of giving Pikachu a massive pair of Pokeballs or endowing Woody with an impressive woody of his own.

One show of our time which was practically begging for a porno version of its own was *Mighty Morphin Power Rangers*, what with its evil sorceress villain, Rita Repulsa, and her trademark chant of 'Magic wand, make my monster GROW!' No imagination required.

Power Rangers was one of a deluge of boys' action shows back then, each series competing to cram in more violence, monsters and general kickassery than anything else on offer.

'Robots in disguise!' became the shout of every young boy caught up in the world of *Transformers*. 'I have the power!' was the choice of *He-man and the Masters of the Universe* fans. Others would declare 'Thundercats, ho!', although I can't remember what particular show that originated from…

Mighty Morphin Power Rangers was the new kid on the block, and my best mate Thomas was into it in a big way. I was never as taken with it, much preferring the daddy of all boy shows, *Teenage Mutant Ninja Turtles*.

Power Rangers revolved around six young fighters who could 'morph' into Rangers, with special powers, superhuman strength and a variety of guff costumes which look like something you would see a group of dickheads wearing on a student night out.

Each had their own 'Zord' - or robot - to pilot and these fighting machines could be combined into one giant 'Megazord' in order to defeat the toughest of enemies and help sell cheaply-made plastic toy versions to gullible kids and their browbeaten parents.

If all of that doesn't sound naff enough, how about the fact that the Mighty Morphin Power Rangers came up against some of the shittiest enemies ever seen on kids' television?

Their aforementioned nemesis, Rita Repulsa, had a hopeless army, the Putty Patrollers, who made for some of the lamest battle scenes ever committed to film.

The storyline went that upon realising her Putty men were being too easily defeated, she created a stronger version, with an iconic 'Z' emblazoned on their chest.

For an added dose of idiocy, these upgraded versions could be defeated just by punching the 'Z' on their chest. This issue was never addressed, and so Power Rangers continued to win battles with ease, simply screaming 'AYAA!' and giving their opponents a good thump in the tits.

Thomas was obviously delighted when they introduced a super-cool new Ranger, with green outfit, called Tommy. Fans of the show instantly loved him. Whenever a bout of imitating *Power Rangers* broke out in the playground, Thomas had instant claim over channelling the spirit of the most awesome character from the show, his namesake.

I still remember vividly how crushed he was when Rita used magic to turn the Green Ranger evil. I got almost as much mileage out of that as I did when my sister Fiona's childhood pin-up, Stephen Gateley, turned out to be gay. My sister's dreams of marriage crushed. My best friend's hero turned heel. Delightful.

(This turn of events would play out again some years later, with an adult Fiona taking a shine to John Barrowman and Thomas' lifelong hero Ryan Giggs turning out to be a mad in-family shagger. Allegedly.)

Not only did that era produce an unrivalled catalogue of televisual gold, its silver screen output was of such high quality that today's offerings are laughable in comparison.

In the modern day, only JJ Abrams' Spielberg-inspired *Super 8* – with its teens who smoke, swear, kiss and generally act like actual kids – can go toe-to-toe with *E.T.*, *The Goonies*, *Ghostbusters* et al.

Everything else in recent years has been lazily-rehashed animated shite featuring vehicles who can inexplicably talk, like *Cars*, *Cars 2*, *Planes*, *Planes: Fire & Rescue*, *Trains 3*, *Trains 3: Part 2*, *Motorbikes*, *Street Sweepers* and *Street Sweepers In Space*. SHITE.

The only good film with a vehicle in its title is *Planes, Trains & Automobiles*, and guess what? That belongs to our era, too.

By accident of birth, kids of the new millennium can't possibly know the joy of paying just a couple of quid a time to enjoy classic films such as *Home Alone*, with the envy of every nineties' child, the Talkboy (imagine the worst Christmas present ever, with which you could record and play back your own voice before realising that the novelty had worn off within one use); *The Goonies*, with its Truffle Shuffle (imagine James Corden trying to shake a spider out from between his tits); or the *Back To The Future* series, with its amazing Hoverboard (imagine a skateboard that, err, hovers)

Our eyes would be out on stalks at the wonderful adventures we were soaking up at the cinema. For a short time, I even believed that the Hoverboard was real.

'How cool would it be if they actually made one of those?' I mused.

My next door neighbour Adam, who was a year older than I, convinced me that a real model had been manufactured to tie-in with the movie, and that the boards were now in production and available for sale.

'Wait here, I'll go in and get mine…'

That anxious wait at the end of his driveway is possibly the most excited I have ever been in my life. It was only after waiting for more than half an hour that I started to have doubts.

Forty five minutes later, he eventually reappeared.

'Well, did you find it?!'

'Find what?'

'Your Hoverboard!'

'Haha, my Hoverboard?! I was having my dinner, you tit. Hoverboards aren't real'.

I was crushed, totally crushed.

However, when it came to getting all green-eyed at a film, *Home Alone* was the king. The Hoverboard trumped the Talkboy and time travel was all well and good, but didn't every little boy of the time go to bed just hoping beyond hope that he'd wake to find his family gone and burglars breaking into his house in the middle of the night?!

I know I spent more time excitedly thinking about that possibility than I did any other film-related fantasy – more time than I spent using coloured straws as lightsabers after the '97 *Star Wars* re-release and certainly more time than I wasted trying to fashion an *Indiana Jones* whip out of my mum's balls of wool.

In preparation of just such an occasion, I started keeping a Super Soaker under my bed, balancing items on top of the door so that they would crash to the floor if it opened, and even went as far one night as to tie a piece of string to my window handle at one end and to my finger at the other so I would become aware of anyone prying open my window through the night.

I started drawing floor plans of our house, writing lists of which toys would be most painful to stand on, and trying to come up with a means of rigging a break-in-activated blowtorch without my mum and dad knowing about it.

Disappointingly, it wasn't to be, and hilariously calamitous robbers never did burgle our family home. I continued to envy Macaulay Culkin until about 1995, when he quietly disappeared from screens completely.

Although *Home Alone* was by far his best, most successful and most popular film, I also have very hazy memories of him in some other films:

My Girl, a film about Macaulay Culkin's romantic relationship with a bee who ultimately decides to murder him.

Getting Even With Dad, starring Culkin as the on-screen son of Ted Danson, an ex-con whose biggest crime is his hideous-looking ponytail.

Uncle Buck, in which Macaulay's character and his siblings get a surprise when their estranged uncle comes to babysit and turns out to be a male deer who excels at making pancakes.

Home Alone 2: Lost In New York, with Culkin reprising his role as Kevin McCallister, new-found friend of pigeon fanatic and football manager, Steve Bruce.

And *Richie Rich*, his last film as a child star, the true story of how Macaulay Culkin was inexplicably given billions of dollars by Michael Jackson to stay quiet and disappear into obscurity.

Macaulay hasn't aged well – he was last seen playing small UK venues with his comedy rock band, The Pizza Underground, ultimately cutting the tour short after having beers thrown at him mid-way through his kazoo solo – but thankfully the films of our generation have. Today's offerings can't hold a candle to the TV and film entertainment that the nineties blessed us with.

No son of mine shall grow up suffering *Open Season 5* when there are perfectly good DVDs of Elliott and his extra-terrestrial chum or the adventures of Leo, Don, Raph and Mikey to binge on. In fact, I might even give him extra homework by insisting he watches them on VHS.

We had finally found salvation, a chance for me to attend to my stomach problems. Off in the distance sat a small cottage.

Looking behind us, there was no sign of our broken-down car. We had come so far that it was no longer visible. Now, there was an end to our quest in sight. I was Frodo, the house was Mount Doom, and I was being driven on by anxious thoughts of a ring: mine.

VII: CHALK DUST TORTURE
'The bell doesn't dismiss you, I dismiss you'.

Kids in the playground would wear the severe scoldings of their teachers like a proud badge – 'terrible behaviour', 'one of the worst classes I've ever taught', 'a punishment exercise for all of you' and so on - but only 102C could genuinely boast 'The worst class in St Mark's history'.

It was a title bestowed upon us by almost every unfortunate educator whose threshold we crossed and one that was hard-earned in the grand scheme of classroom chaos.

102C had the ingredients to make any academy's worst class. It had all the necessary elements: the small handful of poor, worn-down Lisa Simpson types who simply wanted to get ahead in the world; the 'Easily distracted and often disrupts others' kind of idiots like myself, bright but too fond of mischief; the crazy, carefree kids who had no great interest in learning and just enjoyed a laugh; the downright bad boys who would literally stop at nothing to cause chaos; and the easy-target teachers with little to no means of control.

Thirty or so kids came together from different schools,

towns and walks of life to so quickly form one boisterous, horrible band of hooligans, testing the patience of every beleaguered Sir or Madam who was tasked with their collective education.

From day one, we got to grips with our newly-printed timetables and quickly judged which classrooms were prime targets for shenanigans. The answer was almost all of them...

REGISTRATION

Every school day started with Registration. For five years, my mornings began with the company of Mrs. Thomson. All we learned was that what they say about misery and company isn't true.

I was reminded of Thomson when I watched *Monsters Inc.* The slow-talking, dour-faced, miserable secretary slug was a dead ringer for our Regi. teacher.

Big Tam, as we un-affectionately called her, ticked us in each day on the attendance sheet and shared any news or relevant information with us. She did all of this with a foul attitude; evidently she wasn't a morning person.

Often this ten-minute period could set the tone for the whole day. If Big Tam was pissed off, we would goad her and carry on. This could put 102C in just the wrong mood for the rest of the teaching staff.

There wasn't a single day spent in her Registration class where someone failed to shout out 'Queer!' before the person whose attendance was being questioned could respond with the correct shout of 'Here!'

Daryl Allison was usually the protagonist and must have spent more time in the corridor outside her room than he did at the desk assigned to him for those ten minutes. There were occasions where he didn't bother to enter the class, shouting his 'Here!' from the corridor, as he simply skipped the step of actually acting out and just proceeded straight to standing outside the door.

Several bad boys would partake in a bit of dogging (the

plunking school kind, not the sexy car park sort) by attending Registration then sending mates along to later classes with half-baked excuses for their sudden absence from a certain period.

'Oh yeah, Barry got hurt in P.E. – caught his baws a cracker on the pommel horse, I heard. I think he went along to the medical room...'

That my sister-in-law has welcomed me into her family is a minor miracle as for me and my mate Gerry, Registration class was spent constantly kicking the back of Katrina's chair and that of her pal Samantha. With a hard enough nudge of the foot, the chair would swing onto its two front legs against their will, jamming the girls between the chair and the table until we let up. And we did this daily for five years.

She has the patience of a saint, my sister-in-law.

Every day, at some point in every class, someone would swing back on their chair. It usually merited a good nudge forward from the foot of the pupil behind.

Although it drove the teachers bonkers, pupils around the school would regularly set their chairs rocking onto just two legs. Every now and again, there would be a massive, sudden noise and an unexpected scream, then uproarious laughter from all onlookers, as someone lost balance and went crashing to the floor along with their chair.

'And that's why a chair has four legs!' the teacher would cry.

One of the best laughs in Regi. was the day Mrs. Thomson tried to embarrass Daryl. Tired of his poor timekeeping, she once tried to punish him by demanding that he lead morning prayers. Her style of discipline was very much about humiliating the pupil in question and exacting revenge, rather than trying to gently curb the behaviour.

Presumably she thought Daryl would get up in front of class and make a fool of himself through nerves.

Instead, he stood proudly before us all with his hands clasped and head bowed, and led the class through the best prayer session we ever had:

'Alright, God? Hello, big man. Did you watch the Celtic game last night? Of course you did. Great, wasn't it? And what about Henrik Larsson? What a player.

'Anyway, Mrs. Thomson's asked me to do the prayers this morning if that's cool with you, seeing as I was late again. I would say it's because my dad's car wouldn't start, but I suppose you know I only live a couple of minutes along the road so I better not. I'll get on with it.

'God bless Big Tam. God bless 102C, even Craig Scott. God bless my mum, my dad, my wee sisters, my nan, my papa and their wee dog'.

He went on like this for several minutes, with a full classroom of his mates bowing their heads, closing their eyes and trying desperately to stifle laughter.

Mrs. Thomson, meanwhile, sat seething and speechless, hardly able to chastise him for doing exactly as she had asked.

Daryl continued to come in late, but was never asked to lead morning prayers again.

HISTORY

Mr. Campbell taught our class History. I have absolutely no recollection of any of his lessons. My strongest memory of Campbell is finding him and some other teachers blind drunk on the last night of our week long trip to Paris. And who could blame them?

The school trip has to be one of the greatest weeks of any young person's life. Not so much the teachers'.

After eighteen hours on a coach with the smell of rancid farts and the video of *Braveheart* playing on a loop, what delight we took in driving through the red light district of the city. The boys gleefully gave thumbs up to all of the women we saw, and marveled at the window displays of the sex shops we passed.

Students bought playing cards covered in graphic porno scenes that holiday, and we boys would sneak into each other's rooms after curfew to play poker with cards that elicited filthy shouts of 'I'd like to poke her!'

Wullie Collins had the barefaced cheek to approach a magazine stand in the street and ask brazenly for the seller's filthiest skin magazine. God bless the French; the guy sold it to him.

Twenty lads squeezed round Wullie in the middle of a Parisian street for a peek at wild scenes including the only image I've ever seen of a woman sticking a hairbrush up her fanny.

The hotel grew to hate us. The stair bannister broke after bearing too many arses, all of us taking turns to slide down the length of it again and again. The lift was constantly in use; any time we exited it, the buttons for all twelve floors got pressed as a matter of habit.

Opposite the room I shared that week with Gary Parker, Jason O'Rourke and my best pal Thomas was a block of flats. After most of the lads on the trip had bought Class 1 laser pens one night, the four of us retired to our room with Gary's.

The man in the flat opposite us was sat next to a window, happily browsing his computer. At the first sight of a red dot in his dark room, he threw himself down to the floor in a panic, like he feared being taken out by a sniper.

Shaken, anxious and terrified, his little face eventually reappeared at the window as he came up into a cautious kneeling position. Gary landed the red dot on his head perfectly, and at that he sheepishly looked across at the source; four stupid wee boys in the hotel across from his apartment.

He tugged his curtains closed, incandescent, as we fell on the floor laughing.

My mother-in-law talks about how Katrina – my wife's sister, who was also on the trip – would call her folks every night, home sick. My mum still casts up the fact that I didn't phone once during the seven day trip; not even to let them know I had arrived safely. She was equally unimpressed that I returned home with the bar of soap she had bought and packed for me in its original wrapping, untouched.

At least we came home a little more cultured than before. On my first visit to the Sacré-Cœur, I am still proud to report that I didn't bother entering the world-renowned, historical landmark.

Instead, I bought something from one of the dodgy 'looky looky' street vendors outside: a keyring of a gorilla wearing a hula skirt. Incredibly, if you squeezed his stomach, a huge, red boner popped out of the skirt. It was literally the funniest thing I had ever seen.

It was confiscated from me some weeks later as I sat showing off the keyring in Science class, all of us still mesmerised at this little rubber gorilla and his magnificent erection.

The teacher told me that if I wanted it back, I'd have to go and see the year head, Mrs. Cooper. Clearly he didn't believe that anyone would be so bold or so stupid as to ask the terrifying head of year for their sexually-aroused primate toy back. I was, and did. She gave me an unamused 'No' and turfed me out of her office.

HOME ECONOMICS

My wife is confident in the kitchen. I'm not. The reason for that is almost certainly because while she learned how to cook pasta, boil an egg and do other such culinary basics in Home Economics, I made balls out of dough with which to have wild food fights across the classroom.

Periods of Home Eccy, as it was known, were just a full-scale riot for an hour solid at a time. The only way Home Eccy could have been wilder was if we were actually on Eccies.

Every ingredient with which we were trusted was launched across the room as soon as the teacher took her eyes off us for even a second. Eggs. Dough. Flour. Tomatoes. Literally everything.

I have memories of the year head being marched into just about every class I ever took at secondary school, and his visit to Home Eccy to deliver a dressing-down came after Miss Perry got skelped on the back of the head with one of these flying dough balls.

She. Was. Not. Happy.

This habit of going crazy every time Miss Perry looked away got so bad that eventually we moved on from food to utensils. With the Home Economics rooms based on the second floor, we would open the windows and wait for the opportune moment to launch bowls, spoons, chopping boards and anything else we could lay our hands on out to the ground below.

Perry somehow managed to remain oblivious to this until a janitor avoided being struck by an egg whisk by a matter of inches. That was the end of that.

Our wanton destruction didn't end there. That we were allowed to use the ovens is a minor miracle. Copious amounts of self-raising flour were added to oblivious mates' cakes before they were thrust into the oven, causing oversized cakes and much hilarity.

Anything that wasn't nailed down was put in the oven, just to see what would happen, and the temperature dials on ovens were always turned to the maximum setting when the attention of chefs lay elsewhere. No matter what the desired outcome, the oven would always be opened to reveal a black, unidentifiable rock. Smoke billowed out of our Home Eccy class on a daily basis.

Eventually, it was deemed a risk to health and safety and the general wellbeing of the school to allow 102C near the cookery classroom, and we were banned from ever making another molecule of food as long as we were pupils of the school. That was probably just as well, as the

Tupperware box full of each day's produce usually got emptied from the top deck of our double decker bus home, onto the head of some poor nerd passing us on his way home from the town's other school, Kilbrenning Academy.

That they somehow thought we would be safer with sewing machines boggles the mind. That too soon came to an end when someone fed a fellow pupil's tie through the needle feed, with pupil and neck still attached to said tie.

Before long, the rest of our time in Home Economics was spent finding relevant terms like 'Ingredients' and 'Stitch' in a variety of monotonous wordsearches. Paper cuts and airplanes were deemed an acceptable risk in contrast to the heretofore alternatives.

SCIENCE

The school had several Science teachers, with the subject divided into Physics, Biology and Chemistry for third years and above.

I only ever had two of these teachers. For second year Science and for third year onwards for Physics, I had the joy of being taught by Mr. Martin - one of my all-time favourite teachers.

He loved his subject, let his passion shine through in his lessons, taught us loads of fascinating things and peppered the dull lessons with good humour to keep us engaged.

I remember being particularly amused with his 'Come on, it's not rocket science!' gag as we worked on water-powered bottle rockets. That joke was probably as old as the battered textbooks they taught us with, but the class lapped it up all the same.

As a hands-on subject, Science was one of the most popular with us young tearaways. Lessons tended to stick with us due to how much fun was to be had with explosions, fire, chemicals and all the standard fare that came with the subject. This was the one classroom in which explosions, fire and chemicals were actually part of the curriculum and not just things to experiment with when teachers had their back turned.

Despite using up all of its educational value on its maiden appearance in the classroom, the Van De Graaf generator was a staple of the Science classroom. It was the equivalent of the R.E. department's VHS copy of *Sister Act*, something teachers wheeled out as a time-killer when the lesson plans had run dry or a hangover had rendered them incapable of coherent speech.

Having already learned all that the curriculum expected us to know about static electricity, we continued to make use of it purely as a device with which to hurt our friends.

'Hey, come here and see this for a minute…'

ZAP.

'Bastard!'

Just next door to Martin was the room of another teacher in the Science department, Mr. Riley.

He was referred to, perhaps cruelly, as 'Blind Riley', on account of his lack of sight, and to distinguish him from another teacher of the same name.

The stories from his classes were both hilarious and appalling. During roll calls, pupils would shout out 'Here' to cover for absentees. Being a science lab, people would set fire to anything and everything. Even during lessons that were meant to involve only textbooks, tools and chemicals were dragged out and mayhem would ensue amidst a chorus of stifled giggles.

The bravest would dare to test his sense of hearing by trying to sneak as close to him as possible; even gently touching him or flicking his tie.

All of this, in hindsight, is quite dreadful. That the poor man battled on as a teacher in spite of his disability - probably all too aware of much of the nonsense that went on - is very commendable.

I have always liked to tell myself that as a boy who was quite silly and easily lead but basically, deep down, a good and generous person, I wouldn't have done anything of this sort had I been taught by him. I would have taken the moral high ground, I always imagined, and not used his disability as a means for cheap laughs.

In reality, had he been my teacher, I would probably have been up on his desk every lesson. Doing the Macarena. Naked.

My other Science teacher was a man with a simply delightful name, who taught us throughout first year. At the age of eleven, I was taught by a fellow called Mr. Coxhead. At the age of twenty eight, I still find this funny.

The first time I ever saw a list of my soon-to-be teachers' names, I came across Mr. Coxhead and thought it was the greatest practical joke I'd ever seen; that someone had made up an absolutely ridiculous name like Hugh Jass or Mike Hunt and included it in the list for the appreciation of the eagle-eyed. I nearly blew my funny fuse when I discovered that this was an actual man's name and that he really would be teaching me.

In years of being taught by him, Mr. Coxhead's name lost none of its hilarity. None.

He didn't actually cop too much abuse for his moniker on account of the fact that he was a lovely guy. He had a gentle nature, perhaps best typified by the fact that he cycled into school every day on a beat-up old bike that must have been passed down to him from the Victorian era, all in a bid to save the environment, no doubt. It's fair to say that he ran a very relaxed classroom.

For the course of the year that he taught us, he remained absolutely indifferent to the fact that Tony and I would regularly – on what must have been a weekly basis – destroy his pens. Every pen he loaned us was subjected to the flame of a Bunsen burner along its length until the plastic had melted into a series of waves, then was returned to him without comment.

Whether he had a lifetime supply of Bics in his briefcase, I don't know, but he was such an easy-going chap that he never even acknowledged the relentless destruction of his stationery. I like to imagine that to this day, he has a drawer full of pens shaped like the Loch Ness monster which he hands out to the bemusement of any pupil who happens to have forgotten their pencil.

MUSIC

The head of Music, Mrs. Glass, was a small, dumpy woman with a good sense of humour but a short temper.

She was a notorious smoker; how she lasted fifty-five minute periods without a fag is a mystery. The pungent whiff of tobacco was a hallmark of her classroom.

I once borrowed a paperback of Terry Pratchett's *Maskerade* from her after discovering a mutual love of Discworld. Just turning the pages of that nicotine-laden book was like snogging a fifty-a-day chain-smoker as they lay wheezing on their deathbed.

Without a word of a lie, my mum sat down with me for a serious talk on the dangers of cigarettes after coming into my room as I read it. She thought I had given into peer pressure and taken up smoking.

102C was taught by the department's other teacher, Miss Naylor; a far softer touch, and better smelling too.

It was only after I had picked my third year subjects, and no longer had Music lessons, that the two fifty-something Music teachers were joined by the fresh-faced, newly qualified Miss Watson. I dreamt of learning to use my instrument with her expert tutelage…

But alas, we were stuck with Naylor.

Miss Naylor lacked the ability to discipline a class. The fact that she taught a subject that most kids liked, or at least had fun with, counted in her favour. If she had had to deal with the madness of an R.E. period or the sheer hell of a Classics lesson, she would have been signed off with stress within the hour.

As it was, there were several schooldays in which her inability to keep pupils in line were demonstrated.

I remember clearly a lesson in first year when we were each tasked with writing a short song on our keyboard. Instead of experimentally tinkling the ivory waiting for inspiration to strike, I sat gabbing with my new friend Tony Hughes about our favourite moments from *The Simpsons*.

'We drove around until three AM looking for another all-you-can-eat fish restaurant'.

'And when you couldn't find one?'

'We... went... fishing!'

Most of the class were similarly preoccupied. Girls nattered about each other, boys discussed the latest fortunes of Glasgow Celtic Football Club, and the sound of laughter was far more evident than that of musical creation.

At the end of the session, Miss Naylor started to call us up one at a time to test our songs on her keyboard.

With the exception of a few decent kids who had sat patiently amidst the gossipers, quietly writing their little pieces, pupil upon pupil shuffled forward to confess that they had produced nothing. Miss Naylor grew angrier and angrier, moaning furiously at the class for our laziness each time another person came up blank.

Not being in the mood for a bollocking or yet another punishment exercise, I panicked. I knew it was too late to start playing around with my keyboard in a room that had fallen silent but for the wild-eyed ranting of Naylor.

What to do? Could I remember a short segment of a famous song and pass it off as my own? We had recently learned *Mary Had a Little Lamb* *; perhaps I could submit that, or a modified version.

No. That seemed like too big a risk; if I got caught doing that, which seemed likely, I'd be regarded not only as lazy but as a plagiarist to boot, something a music aficionado would surely despise.

---

* B A G A BBB AAA BBB B A G A BBB AA B A G – evidently I've remembered something from school.

There was nothing else for it - I was next. I picked up my pen, thought of the musical notes I knew, and tried to think of some to write down and an order in which to put them.

For reasons I still don't understand, what I wrote was:

'C-A-B-B-A-G-E / C-A-B-B-A-G-E / C-A-B-B-A-G-E'

I stopped writing, looked at the paper and considered what I had just written. Instantly, it seemed a terrible idea, a complete piss-take that would go down like a bear with a sore head being booted in the bollocks.

That's not how it was intended; it was just literally the first thing I could think to do with the musical notes that entered my head.

She called me up just as I was about to score through what I had jotted down. It was too late.

Out of alternatives, I slowly slid my seat back and started the long walk to her desk.

She looked into my anxious face, took the paper from me and examined it for what seemed an eternity.

Eventually, she did the last thing I expected her to: she embraced my vegetable-inspired ditty and started playing it on her keyboard, apparently not realising that the notes spelled out a well-known garden produce.

She finished playing, smiled at me and said: 'Not bad, Graeme. Well done'.

To this day, the 'cabbage song' is the only output of my short-lived musical career. Apparently, taken at face value and played expertly enough, it's 'Not bad' - which, let's face it, is more than you can say for a lot of music written in the latter part of the twentieth century.

Another example of how weak Miss Naylor could be in the face of 102C's notorious misbehaviour was the day she tried to teach us guitar.

Some thirty or so unruly kids were given an acoustic guitar to use for the lesson. Miss Naylor would play a very short, simple bit of music on her guitar and would then lead us through it again as we each played along on our guitar. Like most of our classes, there was actually a short spell where the period went successfully, as per the lesson plan.

The room was hardly filled with the sweet sound of harmonious music, but initially there was at least a definite similarity, for anyone in proximity, between what Miss Naylor was playing beautifully and with our inexpert attempts at copying.

Then someone decided it would be funny to go off-script. Miss Naylor played a few chords and as the rest of the class tried to ape her, one deviant strummed something so strikingly different that it was hilarious, the noise and tempo at which it was played being at complete odds with what the rest of us were doing.

She seemingly wrote it off as unintentional, and continued on. However, it soon became obvious that it was no accident. More and more of us joined in.

Naylor would play something. We would sit, eager-faced, taking it in. Then all at once, we would strum our own mad series of notes, thrashing away at the guitars in complete disharmony with each other.

She stopped playing examples, furious, and started chastising us; at least that's what I assume she did, as the lips on her angry face grew more and more animated. None of us could hear her, over the now-constant barrage of noise that filled the classroom.

I was just getting into Nirvana at the time, and loved how they would often end their gigs with a cacophony of feedback and randomly-strummed notes to create a wall of discordant noise.

That classic image of Kurt Cobain, venomously pulling the strings of his guitar close to breaking point, smashing instruments into speaker stacks and tossing drum parts into the crowd, looks positively tame compared with the chaos we caused. The volume was unbearable.

Eventually she had to give in and just sat there defeated

for the rest of the period, unable to teach over the wall of loud, unrelenting and above all horrible-sounding nonsense that was being wrought from her guitars.

There was also the time that she made the mistake of running an errand for five minutes and foolishly left her keys on the desk. She returned to find she was locked out, peeking through the glass in the door to survey the madness in a state of horror, like a child at the zoo watching the caged monkey pull a turd from its arse.

Filing cabinets gutted, papers strewn everywhere. The instrument cupboard emptied, loud music being fashioned ineptly from all of her instruments as a mosh pit spread out around the players. All of the desks pushed together, with boys taking it in turns to do a running jump off them and into the blackboard with a flying dropkick.

We were 102C, and her mistake was the St Mark's Academy equivalent of a prison guard accidentally sitting his cup of tea on the cell door release button.

PHYSICAL EDUCATION

Short kids and fat kids hate P.E. Thankfully I was tall and skinny, so loved just about every minute of it. While other teachers tried hopelessly to make the rules of trigonometry or the subtle nuances of the French language stick in our minds, all the P.E. teachers expected of the class was that we sorted fair teams for rounders amongst ourselves.

The rest of the school day was a write-off if you were the rounders batter who had your tame hit caught by the opposition, resulting in your whole team having to switch to fielding. Your mum would give you a concerned look that afternoon, as you returned home and went wordlessly to bed...

The scenes of jubilation after a catch were unlike anything else in your school career. Running like footballers to the penalty-taker who has just hit the winner in a Champions League Final sudden death shootout, your teammates would mob you all at once in gleeful elation, celebrating your achievement, before rushing to the batting area to fight over their places in the queue.

King for a day, you walked past the deflated opposition who had just become fielders, straight to the front of the batting line - he who caught the ball always batted first, of that there was simply no question.

Physical Education was always fun, whether the teachers were stupidly trusting us with hockey sticks, stupidly trusting us with javelins, stupidly trusting us with tennis racquets or going for the safe option of athletics. Where there was no equipment needed for activities like 100m sprints or 5K races, it was generally agreed that even we couldn't cause too much damage.

We learned how to do front flips by running at a small trampette and crashing head over heels onto blue sponge mats. That was a skill that came in handy when Mr. McIntyre left us unsupervised in the gym hall for ten minutes one morning. He returned to find all the blue mats shoved together and piled high, as we took it in turns to climb to the top of the twenty foot climbing frame and front-flip off. He seemed more impressed than mad...

We learned how to do social dancing, with the class split into boys and girls and each pupil paired up with a member of the opposite sex. That taught us the moves to one day dance the Gay Gordons at weddings and not a lot else. There was always a surplus of boys, so many a chuckle was had at two lads getting paired together to dance The Dashing White Sergeant.

The rarer-than-rocking-horse-shit opportunity for three minutes of nervous dancing with the sexiest girl in the year (Linsay Burke) just about made up for the munter after munter whose clammy, wart-ridden hands you were forced to hold.

We learned how to correctly start a game of basketball, with a tip-off where one player from each team faced the other and jumped at the referee's say to try and make first contact with the mid-air ball. That made for scenes of humiliation, when George Kerr faced off against his good mate Connor Gallagher. George jumped, Connor never, instead grabbing hold of the waistband of George's shorts at the sound of the whistle. George won the tip-off without contest, realising just around the second that he touched the basketball that he had just leapt out of his shorts and exposed his underwear to his own team, the opposition and both the teams who were sat watching from the benches. Cue hilarity.

At fourteen years old and six foot five tall, basketball was one of two P.E. activities I excelled at. The high jump was the other.

When it came time to record our official athletics and gymnastics bests, I made school history by clearing the high jump at previously unheard-of heights, resulting in my staying behind after the bell until the teacher could finally find a height I couldn't clear. I felt like an absolute champion.

Next week, we were back to football, and my getting relentlessly nutmegged by smaller, quicker players. Why couldn't all sports give advantage to those of a taller build?

My bar-leaping escapades may have made for the greatest ever day of P.E. in my entire school career. The only other contender was the time we did races around the gym hall and I first became aware of a woman's best attributes.

Kerry Barnes had blossomed early and as I sat on a bench at the side waiting for a turn, my mates and I sat mesmerised by the sight of her gigantic knockers swinging from side to side as she ran. Delightful.

Conversely, my worst day came when I forgot to bring my kit, and had to change into the best gear I could cobble together from the basket of unwashed spares. I pulled out a pair of tiny 'hot pants' style shorts, shaking off a pair of crusty y-fronts that had stuck to them, then picked up a t-shirt that was two sizes too small and branded with the logo of a sportswear company that had died out in the 1980s. It was the first and last time I ever forgot my kit.

GUIDANCE

Personal and Social Education some schools call it. Others label it Guidance. We knew it simply as 'Guidie'.

Throughout school, 102C had Mr. McIntyre as our Guidie teacher. He was brilliant: good-humoured, loads of fun, a fantastic counsellor and not nearly as much of a dick as he could have been about how awful our class reports from just about every subject were. He did come down hard on us, but we had a lot of good laughs, too.

His main subject was P.E., so many a Guidie lesson got derailed into a game of rounders.

In fact, very few of our Guidie periods involved the traditional lessons one would expect.

There was the odd alcohol chat. 'Right, own up, who all was getting mad with it at the weekend?'

Occasionally we would be asked to watch some video about drugs. I didn't pay it much attention – something about a guy getting out his bin, talking about brains, getting really hungry and making himself a fried egg. It seemed nice.

But for the most part, he would just talk to us – like young adults, or actual human beings. Ask us what was going on in our lives, in other classes, about what we all wanted out of school. Other times he would just let us talk amongst ourselves – socialise and have a laugh, while he got on with some paperwork or left us alone to go pull some of his other Guidie students out of classes and reprimand them for stuff.

It was a great laugh. Often the chat would turn to jokes.

Our jokes were absolutely scandalous.

As a child then, everyone and anyone was fair game as far as humour was concerned. For many, the abiding memory of the Ethiopian famine crisis is the Live Aid concert and the *Do They Know It's Christmas?* single.

For nineties' kids, what we remember most strongly is not Bono, Bob Geldof or horrific images of starving children that made headline news, but the long-running series of bad taste jokes that followed in its wake.

'How do you save a drowning Ethiopian? Throw him a polo mint'.

When we were growing up, the best jokes were the ones that shocked and appalled; the naughty ones you wouldn't dare tell your parents.

'What's the cruellest thing in the world? Putting an Ethiopian in a circular room and telling him that his dinner is in the corner'.

The Ethiopia gags were the cream of the crop as far as sick jokes were concerned.

'What do you call two Ethiopians in a sleeping bag? A Twix'.

These quips made light of an atrocity in which some of the poorest people in the world were dying terribly and in their millions, often had racist undertones and displayed a basic lack of morality and humanity, yet we swapped them around school like they were innocent 'Knock-Knock' jokes.

'What do you call an Ethiopian with red hair? A matchstick'.

Frankie Boyle would be proud of (or possibly even offended at) the sick one-liners we shared with each other. Any decent adult would look back upon the vast majority of what we did for kicks and said for laughs and be thoroughly ashamed of themselves. Whilst almost all of my childhood memories are fond ones, many of them are now tinged with feelings of regret and guilt.

'How do Ethiopians camouflage themselves? Stand sideways'.

Sick, dreadful, yet somewhere deep in the recesses of my doomed and decaying soul, an inner child still giggles.

When we weren't condemning ourselves to an eternity

in Hell with our awful jokes, we would often break into song. Not in a good-spirited, wholesome sort of way where the class all gathered round, Mr. McIntyre led us in song and we harmonised with each other, but in the same offensive and horrible vein as the jokes we told.

There were ditties about football:

'Oh, my granny played for Scotland / She nearly scored a goal / But she did the splits / And burst her tits / And the ball went up her hole!'

Or, if you were of a certain leaning: 'Aberdeen, Aberdeen, cannae kick a jelly bean / Rangers cannae kick a ball / Celtic are the best of all'.

There were lewd covers of famous songs.

The Bee Gees' *Tragedy* became: 'Tragedy! / When your pants fall down and your bum is brown, it's tragedy!'

Robson and Jerome were in the charts with a cover of *What Becomes of the Brokenhearted*, which we changed to 'What becomes of the man who farted? / All his friends have now departed'.

To the tune of *Scotland the Brave*: 'Here comes the Highland granny / Two big tits and a hairy fanny!'

And a change to the lyrics of *Superstar*: 'Jesus Christ, superstar / Walks like a woman and he wears a bra'.

The children's song *Do Your Ears Hang Low?* was sexualised, becoming 'Do your balls hang low? / Do they wobble to and fro? / Can you tie them in a knot? / Can you tie them in a bow? / Can you throw them over your shoulder / Like a regimental soldier? / Do your balls hang low?'

To the tune of *The Colonel Bogey March*, we sang an old one that went: 'Hitler has only got one ball / Göring has two but they are very small / Himmler has something sim'lar / But poor old Goebbels has no balls at all'. More often than not, the names were changed to those of classmates to suit our purposes.

One popular sing-song question was: 'Does yer maw drink wine? / Does she drink it all the time? / Does she get a funny feeling / When her heid hits aff the ceiling? / Does yer da drink gin? / Does he drink it oot the bin…?'

There were other jibes about fellow pupils – 'I see London / I see France / I see Gemma's underpants', or the classic song for tall folk:

'Skinny Malinky long legs, big banana feet / Went tae the pictures but couldnae find a seat / When the picture started / Skinny Malinky farted / Skinny Malinky long legs, big banana feet'.

Of a similar ilk was 'Hearty Farty went tae a party / And all the wee farts were there / Tooty Fruity did a beauty / And they all ran out for air'.

We must have had farting on the brain, as we also sang 'Beans, beans, the musical fruit / The more you eat, the more you toot / The more you toot, the better you feel / So eat up your beans with every meal!'

Whenever someone did an actual fart – usually a daily occurrence – we would all burst out laughing, or if it was 'silent but violent', singing and joking would give way to arguing about who the perpetrator was through rhyme.

'Aw for fuck's sake, lads, who's fucking dropped one? Was it you?'

'You know what they say… Whoever smelt it, dealt it'.

'Aye, but whoever denied it, supplied it'.

'Whoever did the rhyme, did the crime'.

'Whoever observed it, served it'.

'Whoever sniffed it, biffed it'.

This would continue until we ran out of rhymes or the smell had got too much to bear, and everyone had taken desperate cover in the neck of their jumper.

It's fair to say we didn't get a whole hell of a lot of work done in Guidie. It was an education, but of a very different kind. Some might think Mr. McIntyre could have come down harder on us for the dreadful feedback we were getting from teachers around the school; to that, I would counter that we never once misbehaved in his class. Perhaps he had the right approach all along.

Or perhaps he just really liked appallingly tasteless jokes, songs about granny fanny, and eggy farts.

CLASSICS

Poor Mr. Dawson, our Classics teacher, cut a frustrated, forlorn figure. His necktie was never quite straight, his balding hair always flicked up wildly at one side, and his brow, without fail, was knitted. A career spent dealing with shithead kids was writ large upon the feeble man's disheveled person.

Head of Drama and the school's most senior computing teacher, he was also leader of many after-school clubs and an all-round nice bloke. However, he had two unfortunate features: first was the fact that he taught the deplorably boring Classics, and second was that he bore a passing resemblance to nineteen-seventies' magician Ali Bongo, earning him a nickname that was passed down from generation to generation.

Many a parent had exclaimed: 'Mr. Dawson? Oh, we used to call him Ali Bongo...'

Us nineties' kids, we called Mr. Dawson 'Ali Bongo' not because we understood the cultural reference, but purely because it annoyed him; because class after class after class before us had pissed him off in such a manner, and some traditions were worth maintaining.

It became a subject to be brought up, whispered about, to pass notes on and for the brave - Daryl - to even directly confront Mr. Dawson about.

'Ali... I mean, Mr. Dawson... how come you get called Ali Bongo?'

What need was there to know who Ali Bongo was when you understood that the very mention of his name was enough to send your teacher into a wild, mad eyed rage? His reaction was always that of an angry cartoon character (think Homer Simpson chasing and strangling Bart), a classic outburst with plenty of comedy value.

While in other classes our penchant for mischief was

tempered somewhat by our desire to at least soak up *some* knowledge, Classics was written off as completely useless and given over entirely to nonsense.

To this day, I still know literally nothing about Joan of Arc (I had to Google her for the purposes of this, just to check I had even got her name right) but sixteen years on, I remember reversing the Classics room like it was yesterday. Regrets, I have none.

Mr. Dawson left to run some errand. Leaving 102C unattended very quickly became a thing of the past for teachers, but this was still in the halcyon days of our first few trusted months. An idea spread like wildfire, and by the time he was back we had all turned our desks to face the back of the room.

The desks were of the old-school wooden square variety, just big enough to sit one pupil. The stupidity of the prank and his inimitable reaction sent us in to fits and only served to encourage us.

Instead of complying with his demands that we 'Turn round this instant! All of you!' we simply started banging on the desks like some wild, caged animals, chanting 'We want out! We want out!'

Our class wouldn't need weeks abandoned on an island to become savages: we would touch down and go all *Lord of the Flies* from day one. At times our behaviour was so base and primitive that it's a wonder we refrained from building fires in the hallways or murdering classmates.

You can imagine the rhythmic, booming noises that must have travelled down the corridors as we grew louder and louder with our banging on the desks, chanting for our freedom whilst facing the back wall of the classroom.

Mr. Dawson was pacing the aisles of desks in a fury and I honestly thought his brain was going to explode out of his skull when one more antagonism tipped him over the edge.

Some pupil, presumably out to run an errand or visit the toilet, had decided to check out the source of the noise and popped his head in to cheekily respond: 'You stay in! You stay in!'

Like a matador waving a red flag at a bull, the boy had to be on his toes in order to deal with a charging Mr. Dawson. Off he went, vaulting down the corridor after the boy and bringing us to a crashing crescendo, like the climax to some rock concert encore, as we simply started drumming the desks as hard and fast as possible while screaming 'OHHHHH!'

VIII: SWEET LIKE CHOCOLATE
'I wish you wouldn't eat that rubbish, it'll rot your teeth…'

TWO of my best mates growing up were the Sullivan brothers, Alistair and Andrew. We would spend full days dossing around town getting up to mischief - throwing stones at cow's arses to send them wild, jumping out from bushes to scare younger boys, and climbing onto the roof of their two-storey house just some of our regular misadventures. Despite all of this, some of the locals mistook us for a bunch of soft boys.

That was because we would regularly call in for Lisa and Megan McCarthy, two quiet, prim and proper girls who lived a short walk from the Sullivans' house. The female equivalents of Rod and Tod Flanders.

We would be seen joining them in their garden, visible from the street as it was enclosed by only a short wall, for sweet games of tig, skipping or even pretending to be families in their Wendy house.

Passers-by would give a curious eye to the three mucky boys in grass-stained trousers having happy little tea parties with these most unlikely of female friends.

A common sight during our playdates was the five of us engaged in cheerful rounds of hide-and-seek. Someone would put their hands to their eyes and count to twenty while the others would run off, finding anything for cover within the boundaries of the walled garden. This could go on and on, with the girls and us safely but uncomfortably nestled in our hiding spot for what felt like ages.

That was because the seeker was in fact using this innocent cover as a means for stealing from the girls' older brother.

Brian McCarthy kept his empty gingies stashed around his garden. Gingies (a Glaswegian term) are empty soft drink bottles on which you could collect a money back deposit from shops.

The scheme, which used the returned glass for recycling, generated twenty pence a bottle for any soul brave enough to take the slagging one would suffer for lugging carrier bags full of bottles 'clink-clink'ing through the streets, all for the sake of a couple of pounds.

Collectors would wait until they had a dozen or more empties - enough that you weren't trading in for the sake of loose change but not so much that there was any danger of passing out under the weight of it all - before making the trip to a participating newsagent.

It was never clear why Brian decided that the place to store his collection was out among the girls' toys and his father's petunias. Whatever the reason, Alistair had noticed a few gingies as we passed their house once, poking out from behind some bushes with their unmistakable blue lid and orange labels.

We 'cased the joint' like some would-be jewel thieves, marking it as a decidedly easy job. The first part of our diamond heist master plan was to befriend these girls (who we had thus far barely ever spoken to through years of school) with frequent visits.

As the hiders laid low in their various spots, the seeker would use the opportunity to grab three or four bottles at a time, ferrying them to the street-side of the gate in the wall, placing them just out of sight.

It was never difficult to find other players in the small garden, so after a few stashing trips the seeker would have to hunt everyone down or arouse suspicion.

Almost as soon as we had the full haul - usually within three or four games, each of us taking turns at being the seeker/thief - we would make our excuses and abruptly end the play. We smiled, said our goodbyes and once we were sure the girls were inside and out of sight, we would leg it with their brother's hard-earned collection of ginger bottles.

The nearest store at which we could trade bottles was on the corner of Smith Street and New Street, some five minutes' walk from the scene of the crime. Like any good getaway, we avoided the main roads, and would high-tail it down a lane that took us almost straight from A to B.

We would run the first couple of hundred yards, caught up in the thrill of our heist, then spend the rest of the walk catching our breath, laughing and swapping stories of the robbery, enjoying the feeling of another job gone off without a hitch.

We gave no thought whatsoever to the girls we had just used or the boy from whom we had essentially just stolen money. As far as we were concerned, there were twenty pence pieces (or as good as) lying around in a garden and all we had to do to make them ours was fool some silly girls into playing with us for ten minutes, distract them and make off. Magic. Who cares if the neighbours thought we were a bunch of jessies for playing dolly dress-up? Free money!

Occasionally in church, as confession loomed, I was struck with a pang of guilt at the thought of those Irn-Bru bottles, but that mental tax was a small price to pay for the feeling of elation we experienced every time we started divvying up our share en route to the newsagents.

Our usual take was somewhere between fifteen and twenty bottles, or as much as four quid split three ways. Hardly The Great Train Robbery, but then none of us much fancied having to flee to Brazil.

Even now, with a far greater sense of right and wrong, I struggle to feel too bad about our crime when I recall with such nostalgia the incredible selection of sweets that were the rewards we could lavish upon ourselves with the dirty money. And boy, would our one pound odd stretch a long way in that corner shop.

Confectionary now is a rip-off. Then, our mums would send us to the ice cream van with fifty pence in our pocket to get a can of juice and a sweetie. You would be lucky to get either one with that amount today. Glasgow comic Kevin Bridges is just as dismayed about this as I am. One of my favourite rants of his is on this very topic.

'The final straw for me: I was in a shop and I was buying a packet of Bikers, a packet of Space Raiders and a packet of Johnny's Onion Rings. Now imagine my shock when the guy asked me for *forty five pence*. When 10p crisps are costing 15p, that's when I begin to take an interest in economics...'

Likewise, a gingie bottle back then was worth not just one Freddo or Taz bar but TWO.

If it was a warm day, we would spend our share of the loot on ice poles, lemon Sparkles, Mini Milks, or Screwballs, ice cream with a bubblegum ball inside it for reasons unknown.

Sometimes we would even treat ourselves to a Sonic lolly: ice cream on a stick that looked vaguely like everyone's favourite speedy hedgehog, with gumball eyes, placed in anatomically-incorrect positions, which made him look drunk. The poor bugger would have struggled to escape Green Hill Zone with those cross-eyed peepers, let alone defeat Dr. Robotnik in a boss fight.

Confectioners knew how to lure us in with cheap, sugary gimmicks. We would waste our money (well, Brian's money) on Kinder Eggs, just for the crap toy; Salt & Shake crisps; Push-Pops ('Don't push me, push a Push-Pop' the playground mantra); Double Dips and Dip Dabs; rice paper money; chocolate cigarettes or white candy sticks ('Hey, look at me, I'm smoking!'); sherbet flying saucers, dips or straws.

20p mix-ups full of sugar-laden penny sweets, sold in the distinctive white paper bags, were also popular, full of things like Jazzies, strawberry laces, Mojos, shrimps, mini Jelly Babies, Cola Bottles, Fruit Salads and Fried Eggs.

If you wanted to lose some teeth, you would get stuck into thin, chewy bars such as Wham, Highland Toffee, Dennis The Menace and Irn-Bru. They would turn into a stringy, sticky, wonderful mess without fail.

Some sweets were an experience to be shared in a group. Popping candy was one such treat. Even the terrifying urban myth that drinking too much fizzy cola after a good dose of Fizz Wiz would cause your stomach to explode did nothing to stop us downing the stuff (just as we listened wild-eyed to the myths that some psychopath was lacing Halloween candy with drugs or hiding razorblades in it, then went out on October 31st all the same).

Eye Poppers were another favourite for eating with mates. Watching your chums as they tucked into the incredibly sour bubblegum was always a great chuckle. The same could be said for Atomic Fireblasts, a hard candy with a bizarre, disgusting, hot flavour. Everyone would have to 'do' theirs at the same time and you would all fall into fits of laughter at the look of disgust etched upon every face.

Dolly beads were perhaps the ultimate sweet to be bought with pals. You would all get a bracelet full of beads then run around outside the shop garnering 'tut's from passersby, nervously dodging tiny sweet after tiny sweet as they pinged around furiously, always in danger of thumping some poor sod in the eye. Great fun, although there was always the threat of lining up a target to fire only for the bead to somehow ping backwards and agonisingly rattle your tooth.

Meanwhile, behind the shop counter would be row upon row of clear plastic tubs full of sweets you could buy in quarter-pound bags. Soor Plooms, strawberry bon-bons, rhubarb and custard or strawberry and cream chews, and little lumps of Edinburgh Rock were all favourites of mine.

Some of the best sweets of our childhood are no longer available. Thankfully, Cadbury brought back Wispa, but there has been no such return for Secret, Nestle Quik bars, Marble, Taz, Crispy M&Ms, Squeezit juice, Toffos, Fuse, Astros, Polo Citrus or Campino.

Also long gone are the fizzy soda drinks released as a tie-in to *The Simpsons* at the peak of its popularity: cans of D'oh Bad Apple Krush, Blues, Krusty Kola, Cherry Bomb Cola, Manic Mallow, and Itchy and Scratchy.

Willy Wonka's Nerds have also been discontinued in the UK, although mercifully they are still available to buy in some quarters.

One of the biggest thrills for us candy-obsessed children was the appearance of the ice cream van. Even better, a 'new' van that wasn't your street's usual visitor was enough to send the neighbourhood's kids into a frenzy.

The queue would stretch as far as the eye could see if, instead of the usual van (proclaiming 'DON'T SKID ON A KID' alongside a crap painting of a mouse with big black ears bearing such a poor resemblance to Mickey Mouse that Disney hadn't bothered taking legal action), a mysterious new van appeared (with a child-like painting of four mystery-solving teenagers and their brown dog emblazoned on the back, alongside a 'HAVE AN ICE DAY' slogan).

The incredibly rare outing of the fish and chip van would make people properly lose their shit.

In addition to a wonderful selection of the above sweets, the ice cream van could also be visited for the procurement of something much more dodgy and nefarious.

No, not drugs: Glasgow's Ice Cream Wars thankfully never made it down to Ayrshire. Instead, we were able to buy caps for our cap guns and fun snap bangers, both cheap toys with which you could terrify the local old women.

Ice cream in one hand, bangers in the other, we would run about on summer nights making a happy nuisance of ourselves.

With so much choice on offer, all of this gave us, quite literally, food for thought: what would we spend our ill-gotten quid or two on? How far could we make it stretch?

Pretty damn far, was usually the answer. Gingie bottles traded in and hands totally full of treats, we would hunker down on a pavement kerb and not move until we had polished off our unjust rewards.

Looking back, we would put away a ridiculous amount of sugary crap in one sitting: picture Milhouse Van Houten tripping out after his all-syrup Super Squishy or Bart and Lisa groaning atop the mountainous pile of sweetie samples pinched from the Candy Convention for an idea of just how gluttonous we got.

This scenario played out with shocking regularity. Thieves love easy pickings. Robbers have been known to hit the same spot again and again if the job continues to be a sure thing: we were no different. Brian continued to collect gingie bottles, continued to store them in the McCarthys' garden and we, for our part, continued to half-inch them in order to load up on sweet candy goodness.

Alas, all good things must come to an end. The day we had been dreading eventually came.

'Hi, Lisa. Are you two coming out to play?'

'Just a minute', she said, closing the door almost fully. I thought I had detected a slightly strange tone to her voice, a nervous look upon her face, but dismissed the thought almost instantaneously.

There was some excited chatter amongst us three, hushed conversation and speculation about how much we each thought today's haul might amount to, as we stood waiting on the steps.

Then came the sound of footsteps from behind the door, growing louder, a large figure appearing silhouetted through the frosted glass panels on the door, coming towards us.

It swung open to reveal their father, at that moment the tallest man in the world.

Our eyes collectively widened, jaws froze.

'The girls will not be coming out to play today'.

We understood 'today' to mean 'ever again you little shits, now get off my property before I kick you in the balls'.

In the background, before promptly about-turning from the doorstep, I noticed Brian lurking further down the hallway. Having obviously been told 'I'll handle this' by his father, he stood itching to see what was to be done to these heinous criminals who had so cruelly helped themselves time and time again to his gingie stash without remorse. This was his day in court. He wanted to see the moment where we were metaphorically led off in handcuffs, see us brought to justice.

I am not a little ashamed to say that we did not leave immediately. After the door slammed shut, we had the nerve to quickly scour the garden for any sight of ginger bottles, and left only when we realised the stash had been relocated, that one last raid was not to be. We had no shame whatsoever.

I am happy to report that my life of crime is no more, that I am now some twenty years clean. For more than two decades, I have not stolen a thing, least of all some poor kid's gingie bottles.

IX: THE MASSES AGAINST THE CLASSES
'It's your own time you're all wasting'.

To say it was difficult to keep 102C under control would be an understatement. It would be easier to nail jelly to a wall.

Lunchtime was presumably the highlight of the school day for our teachers; an hour of peace, time enough to square things up, bolt other things back down, have a quick cry into their pile of jotters and brace themselves for the afternoon:

'Only another couple of hours to go. Come on. I can do this!'

Meanwhile, pupils would be enjoying one of three options for lunch.

The first was a packed lunch, generally a guaranteed source of teasing. Imagine your parents loving you enough to make you sandwiches and provide you with snacks. 'PUSSY!'

The second option, a school meal, would be paid for with your swipe card, which you would pre-load with credit at the swipe card top-up machines.

One memory of the 'swipies' that still really amuses me

is the day that one top-up machine broke; rather than swallowing an inserted pound coin, the machine was spitting it back out but crucially still counting it as credit. Word very quickly went round the school and soon the lunch hall was queued out with hordes of pupils waiting to abuse the system; the first and only time in the school's history that people were queueing for a chance to use the swipies.

The dodge got brought to a stop when the dinnerladies noticed something amiss. With a bit of intelligence on our behalf, the scam *could* have flown under the radar indefinitely. But predictably, pupils hadn't had the foresight to only blag themselves an amount of stolen credit small enough that it would go unnoticed: most pupils had sunk the same pound coin in so many times that their credit amount was just ludicrous.

Two boys in our year, Wullie and Adam, got themselves suspended after topping up with sixty pounds of credit. Sixty pounds! What parent in their right mind would send their child in with that sort of money for lunch? In coins, no less!

'There you go son, there's three score for lunch. That'll do you for the next four months or so.'

The other alternative for lunch was to bounce into town in anticipation of a 'square-go' with our rival academy which almost never came to fruition, a pizza crunch from the local chippy and enough sugary junk that we could practically fly back to school for more of the same.

'Round Two: FIGHT!'

ENGLISH

The English department was staffed with the following teachers:

Mr. Jordan, the department's notorious joker, of whose lessons kids told happy, hilarious stories; predictably, our class was never taught by him.

Mrs. McLeod who, for reasons covered previously, allegedly took to drink.

Mrs. Miller, an old-school teacher so long in the tooth she doubtless still believed in corporal punishment; hell, she would have given capital punishment a go if she thought she could get away with it.

Miss Richards, a crabby fat woman who was crabbier than a giant crab stuffed full of crabs-ridden crabs eating crab sandwiches.

Mrs. Martin, the despot who so cruelly inflicted Lewis Grassic Gibbon's *The Sunset Song* * on us in fifth year.

Mrs. Milne, who must have thought I was some fresh-air addicted freak; come rain, shine or snow, the window next to my desk in her classroom got opened every day without fail. That woman smelled like a family of rats had crawled up her arse and had a farting party before they died.

And Mr. Currie, who probably still lives in fear of becoming the subject of a police investigation…

On an afternoon that will live in infamy, we traipsed into Mr. Currie's class full of lunch and in no mood for English. We wanted an easy period. Apparently so too did Mr. Currie; he was prepared to offer us a reward for good behaviour.

This was, in fact, how he lost control of the class.

On the face of it, a bribe for an easy period seemed a good idea. The problem was that he had obviously made the same offer to all that day's classes - and some prankster had stolen his parachute, leaving him freefalling with only a rucksack full of dirty laundry.

He had presumably written said reward on his whiteboard earlier in the day, as a reminder and incentive for his hard-grafting pupils to work towards. Perhaps it

* First line of the blurb: 'Faced with a choice between her harsh farming life and the seductive but distant world of books and learning, Chris Guthrie eventually decides to remain in her rural community, bound by her intense love of the land'. If that alone doesn't make you want to burn down the world's libraries, what will?

had said 'CHOCOLATE' or 'WATCH A FILM'.

However, some miscreant had rubbed out his writing and replaced it with a reward that gave the offer a very different tone indeed.

'Good afternoon, 102C. Nice lunch? I hope you're all well. If you could all get your jotters out, pens on the desk, I have an offer to make you.

'We have some hard work to get through in this period, but I'd appreciate your cooperation. If you behave, there's something in it for you. Be good today, and I'll give you the treat that's up on the board...'

I thought I was going to be sick with laughter. Each time I regulated my breathing, I would catch the look on another pupil's demented, hysterical face and we would all double over with hilarity once more.

Mr. Currie had turned red, his poor face bearing a look of abject shock, as he stood with hands on hips and surveyed a whiteboard that read simply: 'A WANK'.

TECHNICAL

Our class were taught Techy by Mr. Andrew, a notoriously odd fellow whose every practical demonstration ended with 'And Bob's yer auntie!'

The line never lost any of its humour, as it never had any to begin with.

I had great fun knocking out some of the jaggy-edged crap I produced, most notably a *Legend of Zelda* mail holder and a *South Park* pencil case, all of which still takes pride of place in my mum's house.

When we weren't ham-fistedly carving out guff trinkets or filing our fingernails down on the electric sanders, the rest of our time in Technical was spent throwing the set-squares and compasses into the ceiling tiles to see if they would stick, or ruining the school uniform of some poor sod. Nails would be dipped in glue and thrown at the back of some unsuspecting victim, whose mother would soon be writing an angry letter to the headie.

Tech was also the class in which Craig McDonald very nearly knocked what little sense I had out of me. I had taken a handheld brush, held it to my crotch and announced to him in front of the class: 'This is yer maw's hairy bush!'

He spent the next five minutes chasing me around the room in a murderous rage while I, perpetual shitebag, ran away from him and pleaded for forgiveness.

In hindsight, being twice his height, I should have just stood my ground and battered him with the wooden side of his mum's fanny.

FRENCH

For me, secondary school put paid to the old adage 'Cheats never prosper'.

Teachers could have rewarded the innovation and cunning that was invariably involved in conning our way through secondary school exams, essays and everyday lessons. Cheats prospered often, provided they never got caught.

Sometimes, it involved blind luck. Take, for example, our Maths exam.

An adult would sit in on every exam to fill the role of invigilator. This essentially involved making sure no one was cheating, be it by writing answers on the side of their rubber or sneaking in notes within the pages of their little French dictionary.

Our year hit it lucky when the elderly guy invigilating our Maths exam fell asleep. Throughout rows and rows of desks, pupils hurriedly spun round to ask friends what they had written down as answers, rushing to fill in any blanks on their paper before the old boy left the land of nod.

Other times, hard work went into cheating. For an English assignment in which we were to write an overview of a subject we were passionate about, I chose 'The history of Nintendo' and copied an article from that month's *Nintendo Official Magazine* word-for-word.

It took me hours, as I handwrote and reproduced thousands and thousands of words verbatim. I even had the cheek to cut out pictures from the piece and glue them in. What I passed off as my own essay – actually the work of a professional, salaried journalist - was held aloft as a glowing example of what could be achieved in our English class.

Others got caught at the same game – my mate Ken lazily copied and pasted something from a gaming news website for a Computing essay, resulting in one of his paragraphs opening with the line 'We've got the scoop!' Teacher was not amused.

From day dot, an incredible level of dishonesty started creeping into pupils, many of whom had never before cheated in their life. We had stepped into the Garden of Eden. In our maiden days at St Mark's, an excited whisper went round the playground: 'The answers are at the back!'

And we ate from that tree of forbidden fruit with shocking regularity.

Secondary school textbooks the world over are made with a level of wholly misplaced trust – that by their teens, pupils can be counted on to willingly solve questions put to them, then use the answers provided only as a means of verifying that their work is right.

The excitement of discovering those answer indexes was incredible. In fact, it actually took you by surprise to learn that the teacher was in on this; at first it was assumed to be some massive, incredible secret.

They *knew*?! What were they thinking?

We tripped ourselves up amidst that initial clamour for instant, easy answers. Maths solutions would be submitted without working. Children who had never previously excelled at a given subject were suddenly blasting through pages of work with perfect tens. If a list of answers had so much as one error and you made the mistake of copying it, the teacher blew your cover in an instant.

Teachers cottoned on fast. Of course, they must have

faced this initial clamour for fast and easy answers every year. Perhaps we were too hasty in writing them off as morons.

It soon became apparent that we would have to be smart with the very loophole which was preventing us from becoming smart. Sums and questions would be assessed for difficulty and those which looked least taxing would be tackled head on. Only the problems that required any mental taxation were subject to a quick textbook flick. The odd incorrect answer would be thrown in on purpose, with working provided to show where we had gone wrong, just to throw teacher off the scent.

In time, the thrill of those indexes wore off. Pinching answers from the back became standard. Minimal effort was commonplace.

To truly cheat the system involved imagination.

Take my mate Gerry, and the time he found himself king of French for a day with an ingenious plan that involved such expert preparation and perfect execution that it's a miracle he didn't go on to become a bank robber.

He and I sat at the back of French class for lessons with the diminutive demon that was Mrs. Bennett, swinging on our chairs, annoying (read: flirting with) the girls who sat in front of us, and generally failing to learn French.

As with much else throughout school, it was a question of interest. I, regrettably, had no interest at that age in learning a language, a flaw I am paying for to this day.

So instead of learning one of the most beautiful languages in the world, Gerry and I sat as far from the blackboard as possible, discussing the new Eminem record and working on a plan to see the great Slim Shady in concert someday, like a couple of morons.

(However, I am pleased to report that I won tickets for Gig On The Green that year in Glasgow, gave my second ticket to Gerry and we did indeed see Eminem, probably on a night when we should have been doing French homework.)

The cry was usually: 'What do I need to learn French for? I'm never going to go to France!'

Of course, I have since been twice and love the country – and its people, food and cinema – but twelve year old me could not possibly imagine needing to go to a country full of 'cheese-eating surrender monkeys'.

The sheer scale of our stupidity is perhaps best demonstrated by the fact that one morning, upon realising I had forgotten to do a French homework assignment, I spent the first five minutes of our period looking up how to say 'Le chien a mangé mon devoir' – or 'The dog ate my homework' – as an excuse, in order to garner a big laugh. I was now learning French in order to avoid learning French.

Then came the exam in which Gerry pulled off his great feat.

I took the scenic route to Mrs. Bennett's French class that morning – going the long way round, via unnecessary trips to the toilet and the vending machines to kill time – all in an attempt to delay suffering a period in which I knew I was not only being asked to write out a five hundred word French essay from memory, but do so without Gerry's company and inevitable, amusing distractions.

Gerry was off school, as I had learned in morning registration. One of the boys from the Kilbirnie bus explained that he was ill. So that was it; I would face this horrible written exam on my own.

We had been working on the content of this exam for a while, writing out our essays a couple of times in an attempt to drill them into our minds. Mrs. Bennett had cast her eye over them and gave us feedback on how we had fared in our first attempts.

Now, today, we would try to recreate our essay word for word without being allowed a copy of our practice attempts. We had been asked to memorise our five hundred word essays. It was time to see how much of them we had retained.

For my part, I managed well enough: in fact, parts of it I had remembered letter for letter, word for word, without actually being able to say what the sentences meant. Having looked at the essay countless times, I had managed to photographically memorise the order of the letters and words, but not their meaning when put together. The point of the exercise had perhaps been lost on me.

We handed our essays in and that was that, exam finished.

No one, not even the teacher, seemed to give any thought to the fact that there was one pupil still to pass.

When he reappeared the next day, Gerry seemed almost like an afterthought for Mrs. Bennett. Clearly, he still had to do the exam, but with a class full of pupils moved onto something else, Gerry's need to partake in yesterday's lesson seemed to be the last thing on Mrs. Bennett's mind.

As part of his masterplan, Gerry had banked on just that. Just as he had assumed would happen, Bennett asked him to take his pen and paper through to a small room further down the corridor, away from the rest of the class so that he could remain distraction-free.

He left, but not before slyly breaking the magician's code, showing me the secret to one of the greatest tricks I have seen to this day: he had taken his practice essay, which Mrs. Bennett had previously given the thumbs up to, and copied it out word for word onto a tiny piece of paper. This scrap of paper was so small that it could be sellotaped discreetly to the palm of his hand, yet he had somehow managed to fit all five hundred words onto it in the smallest handwritten font imaginable.

When he was finished and had received his near-perfect mark, I asked him to stick his palm in the air (piece of paper and all) and high-fived him in view of Mrs. Bennett.

She was still none the wiser.

That was the highlight of a detested subject in which we had to make our own entertainment.

One way of doing so involved the dictionary. Across the country, school pupils were given wee pocket-sized French dictionaries with which to check translations. Whoever oversaw the production of these little books (perhaps the same chap who had put answers at the back of our textbooks?) seriously overlooked or underestimated the hilarity that can be caused by the foreign equivalents of swear words.

'Merde! Nique ta mere! Chatte! Bâtard! Salope! Putain!'

We would turn the air (sacré) bleu, sitting at the back of the class and loudly uttering some of the very few French words that have stuck with me in the years since I left school.

Many teachers were wholly undeserving of the 'merde' we gave them. However, French seemed to be a subject taught only by the most twisted and hated individuals that the staffroom boasted. French teachers were downright evil, completely failing to illicit feelings of guilt or remorse even now. They deserved everything we gave them.

Mrs. Bennett was less than five feet tall, so probably had 'small man syndrome' – that explained why she was a complete bitch. Mr. McIntosh had a chronic (and hilarious) dandruff problem and over-eye caterpillars that earned him the school-wide nickname of 'Eyebrows', which doubtless contributed to his foul demeanour. Mrs. McAuley patrolled the corridors like a guard in a Nazi concentration camp, had a voice that could frequently be heard booming round the hallways and was alleged to have thrown a chair across the classroom on more than one occasion, yet was arguably the least-hated of the French teachers, which said it all.

'Eyebrows' was one of the easiest teachers to wind up. His buttons were neither hard to find nor difficult to push.

One afternoon in our first week of secondary school,

Mr. McIntosh disappeared into the cupboard to grab some resources and reappeared to discover his whole lesson plan gone from the chalkboard. Keith Smith had run up while he was indisposed and wiped the whole thing off.

Another day saw someone put chewing gum in the lock of his classroom door, leaving him standing in the corridor going apeshit while passersbys tittered and his pupils enjoyed an afternoon locked out of class.

Likewise, he once ended up locked inside his classroom after leaving his keys out in plain sight, within the grasp of wandering hands and mischievous minds. He was reportedly seen by many amused classes clambering through his window and into the internal courtyard of our square school building before sheepishly chapping on the window of the head teacher's office to get back in.

That same window of his was a target of my friend Gerry and I on one morning spent in a classroom above and at ninety degrees to his. We spent much of the lesson pelting his window with Skittles, before he eventually realised the source and burst into our room unannounced to rain down merry hell on us both. One trip to the year head's office later and I had lost whatever was left of my packet of Skittles.

A perk of senior teaching staff, presumably: eating confiscated sweeties.

I have no idea how it started, but it somehow became tradition for any hoodlum daring enough to bang his classroom door upon passing. Many a lesson was interrupted by a sudden 'BOOM!' sound as a fist met the outside of his door.

He became so used to it that his reflexes were actually pretty sharp; within seconds of the sound, he would be tearing out the door and screaming after the miscreant responsible.

While many teachers were targeted for mischief just for the fun of it, 'Eyebrows' actually deserved the nonsense which he had to put up with, on account of being an evil, spiteful, permanently angry git, and humourless to boot. He was about as twisted as a set of headphones produced from a trouser pocket.

In return for the horrible way he would treat us, we would burst into fits of coughing and humming to test his patience, or tease him about his dandruff by asking 'When was it snowing, Sir?'

My finest moment of flake-taunting came one day I found his home address on some staff paperwork and used an offer at the time on headandshoulders.com to send him a free sample of anti-dandruff shampoo.

102C loved being taught French by 'Eyebrows' and always took great pleasure in the furious outbursts we managed to provoke from him. We didn't think a teacher more easily irritated existed, until Mr. McIntosh was off one day (perhaps getting corrective surgery done on his flaky scalp) and a legend by the name of Mr. Paton stood in.

We only had him for a few days, but those were some of the greatest days of my school life.

As a means of testing him out - as we always did with newbies - we all spent the beginning of his first period putting pencils on the ends of our desks and karate chopping them across the classroom.

Straight off the bat, he went from zero to ten: from mild-mannered to apoplectic with rage. Bullseye.

We soon started humming, and that was when we realised what a wonderful time we were going to have with this man as our teacher. Wild-eyed and spitting at the mouth, he tried to silence us by shouting out the sound 'PSHT!'

As 'shoosh' sounds go, it was the strangest any of us had ever heard. Where the 'p' had come from, no one knew. The more noise we made, the louder he repeated that wonderful noise – 'PSHT!' – over and over again. It grew funnier with each uttering.

Soon the whole classroom of pupils was echoing the

sound back to him. A game of verbal Psht Tennis broke out.

'PSHT!'
'PSHT!'
'PSHT!'

He became angrier and angrier. Desperately wanting us to stop, he became even more serious about shooshing us – by repeating the word 'PSHT!' even louder, trying to shout it over the sound of twenty-odd pupils also shouting 'PSHT!'

It was farcical, one of the funniest afternoons I ever spent in a St Mark's classroom. This chaos played out for a good fifteen minutes or more.

Eventually, Mr. Paton completely lost the rag, and unexpectedly slammed both his hands down hard and **incredibly** loudly on the desk.

It was fucking terrifying. The whole classroom went silent in shock and awe, as his sudden physical outburst jarred us into speechlessness. He had finally achieved what he had been so comically trying to do, and had successfully shooshed the entire class.

That silence lasted only for a couple of seconds until, as if to reinforce what he had been trying to say and underline that he had had the last word in his request for silence, he went:

'PSHT!'

He lost us, completely and utterly lost us. For the next few minutes, every pupil in the class went red, unable to even shout back a mocking 'PSHT!' in reply as we all struggled to breathe with laughter.

The next two days in his classroom were spent shouting 'PSHT!' for fifty-five minutes at a time. Mr. McIntosh soon returned, and discovered that the class had developed a new, much-loved catchphrase in his absence.

ART

Art class was five years of drawing and painting shit

under the tutelage of Mrs. Malone, a crabbit old chainsmoker with whom I had a love/hate relationship. We fought like cat and dog, passionately arguing over the minutiae of art - whether a little tree belonged in the corner of my line drawing, or the eyes were too close together on my latest portrait.

She would regularly frighten the class with wild-eyed rants at me, and I once stormed out of her classroom after a disagreement over whether there was too much yellow in the painting I was working on.

I loved her, the crazy old bag.

In my senior years of Art class, I met Jennifer: a sixth year who I started dating in September 2002, proposed to four years later, married after six and started a family with some eleven years after we met in Art.

Art was good.

MATHEMATICS

Mrs. Merritt finally won us over some five years after she started teaching us Mathematics. After years of taking our shit, she announced to the class apropos of nothing: 'I can solve a Rubik's Cube really quickly'.

Once we had had a few seconds of wondering where the hell that outburst had come from, the face of every pupil in the room screwed up as if to say: 'Bullshit'.

And at that she was off, producing a Rubik's Cube from her desk drawer, showing us all that the tiles were currently scrambled up in no particular order, then racing her way through click after mesmerising click, until no more than two minutes later, she was able to hold aloft one solved Rubik's Cube with a modest little look on her face.

It was one of the most amazing, random sights I saw in my five years of secondary school. There was a standing ovation, and with that Mrs. Merritt had won the respect of a class she had had no end of mischievous nonsense from.

Five years earlier, we had discovered that she had a

serious dislike of Tippex.

One morning, early in our time at St M's:

'Is that Tippex I see?'

Every head looked up, wondering what would prompt such an outburst in a silent classroom.

The owner of the error-correcting fluid and the now centre-of-attention looked a bit sheepish as he managed a little 'Err, yes?'

'Ooooooooh, I really, really don't like Tippex!' seethed Mrs. Merritt. 'I'm going to have to take it off you'.

Everyone was a tad bemused by the whole thing and soon returned to work, thinking nothing else of it for the time being.

A week or so later, after the fifth or sixth such Tippex-related scolding, it had officially become a matter of 'bam up', something with which to instantly infuriate and wind up our Maths tutor.

'Mrs. Merritt, I've made a wee mistake here. Got any Tippex I can borrow?'

Pupils would be on the lookout for the offending item on the desks of others. As soon as a little tub was innocently produced from a pencil case, a cry would go up: 'Hiy, Katrina Darroch, is that Tippex I see? Mrs. Merritt doesn't like Tippex!'

It became a real occasion in the class when Mrs. Merritt spotted an offender and called the person on their stationary misdemeanour.

'Is that Tippex I see, young man?! I really don't like Tippex!'

The whole class would join in, rounding on the shamefaced individual, pointing and chanting:

'Tippex! Tippex! Tippex!'

The day that someone raided Mrs. Merritt's top drawer and dished out every confiscated tub so there was a Tippex pot on the desk of every pupil in the class made for a scene reminiscent of the sequence in *Hook* where a terrified Captain Hook hears ticking and flips out, smashing every clock in sight.

Her other real dislike was for pupils preparing to leave her class before being told to.

Five minutes before the period-ending bell, pupils would enter stealth mode, discreetly packing items into their bag. People would ever-so-gently slide their arms into the sleeves of their jacket then zip it up with all the care one would handle a bomb with.

An angry cry would disrupt proceedings: 'It's not time to pack up yet! Get your jackets off and pencils back on the desk, 102C!'

'What about my Tippex, miss, will I get that back out too?'

MODERN STUDIES

In Pamela Stephenson's biography of her husband, the comedian and my hero Billy Connolly, there's a great line that explains how he and his workmates would trick their gaffer into letting them skive:

'When they were fed up welding, they would seduce him with his own nostalgia'.

We had two teachers with whom we could do the same. Our Maths teacher, Mr. MacPherson, would take almost no encouragement to go off on a tangent about Celtic Football Club, reminiscing about his team's past glories or that weekend's results and ensuring that the rest of the lesson involved no mathematics beyond score lines.

Likewise, our Modern Studies teacher, Mrs. Traynor, would deviate from her subject for a trip down memory lane, a discussion on last night's telly, or just about anything else we could throw at her.

As a last resort, we could goad her into ranting about politics. While it was still relevant to Modern Studies, listening to her moan about what a shower of charlatans the Westminster MPs were was at least better than doing any work which involved engaging our brains.

Our other Modern Studies teacher, Miss Lyons, was

even easier to distract. It took her weeks, maybe even months, to realise that the reason her television kept behaving strangely was because Daz Mitchell had a fancy new watch that could double as a remote control. With a bit of fine-tuning to set it to the right frequency, the watch could control any television it came near.

Many, many Modern Studies lessons were interrupted by the television seemingly turning itself on at random, flicking channels, increasing and decreasing in volume, and shutting off again – only for the same thing to happen again later. We lost count of the number of times she tried changing the batteries in her remote control over those weeks.

Miss Lyons looked properly spooked every time the television had another 'episode'. Towards the end of her time in the dark, just before she learned of Daz and his watch, she became so distracted at each flicker of the television that the lesson was effectively a write-off from that point on. I think she genuinely started to believe in ghosts.

Television-addicted ghosts.

COMPUTING

Every time the Computing teacher left the room (it's a wonder any of them ever did), everyone would rip keys off their computer's keyboards. These would then be placed back on in a new order. There would be shouts of 'Right, who needs a W?' - we had all decided on a phrase to spell and needed extra letters with which to do it.

On teacher's return, there would be rows of keyboards that instead of the usual QWERTY setup, would have a top line that read 'UR A WANK', 'JOBBIES' or 'FUCK YOU'. Glorious.

The hard balls inside our computer mice were also fair game for removal: one of them launched at your head could knock the last fortnight's Computing lessons out of your brain.

At the long, wall-length desk of computers, I sat next to my friend Gerry.

To the right of us was Trevor Brown, to the left Ken Ho. The former was dumber than a bag of especially dumb hammers. His daily requests for help or answers could genuinely be fobbed off with gobbledygook: he would ask me for help with his Visual Basic coding, so I'd turn to him and quietly say something like 'Fizzuboofa blum dwah' in a tone that suggested I knew what I was talking about, nodding and pointing sternly all the while. He would happily accept this as an answer and return to his work. Last time I heard what 'Bruno' was up to, it did not surprise me to learn that he was not a qualified brain surgeon, or mathematics professor.

The latter, wee Ken, lost countless essays after Gerry and I discovered that pushing the 'Windows' key followed by L and Y would log his machine off without saving his work.

We became so adept at speedily hitting those three keys on Ken's keyboard that his computer could be logging off and taking his hour's work with it before he even knew what was going on.

It got to the point that the poor bugger had to hunch over his keyboard, head practically touching the keys, with his right arm wrapped round it like a protective barrier, while using his only free hand to slowly tap away at his essays.

RELIGIOUS EDUCATION

R.E. lessons would involve the TV unit being wheeled in – followed by at least ten minutes of technical meltdown for teacher, an inevitability for any adult when attempting to use even the simplest technology in front of a room full of people – with one of three videos then getting fired into the VCR player: *Sister Act*, *Sister Act 2: Back in the Habit* or *Cool Runnings*.

The first two at least had a loose religious connection

with their singing nuns. If there was a theological undertone to the story of Jamaica's bobsled team then I missed it, despite our repeat viewings.

Some days we would get vaguely on-topic, as a colouring-in sheet depicting Jesus dishing out dozens of fish and Hovis was flung at us. We were expected to colour quietly for the guts of an hour. Amidst the soft noise of worn-out felt tips scratching across paper, the only other sound in the classroom was the occasional groan of 'Are we not watching one of our films today, Miss?'

One R.E. teacher, Mr. Wilson, was also tasked with a bit of sex ed. Who could forget the day he sat us down and explained the contraceptive 'pull out' method? No awkward demonstrations of whacking a condom on a plastic stiffy at our Catholic school. Just pull your member out at the cusp of the best bit and you'll be fine.

Mr. Wilson assured us that this had only failed him and his wife four times, producing four children.

Billy Connolly said it best: 'At the point of ejaculation, wild horses couldn't make me go in that direction!'

Those super-rare occasions when our R.E. teacher was brave enough to actually try to teach us R.E. would sometimes involve visits to the oratory, the school's prayer room. This was a small square room with soft carpets, cushions for sitting on, low lighting, a cassette player for calming music, and little else, intended for silent reflection and group prayer. We loved it, as the cushions made for great pillow fights.

No sooner had we tiptoed into the oratory (barefoot or in socks, as the teacher had asked us to take our shoes off) than we were marched back to class after yet another wild cushion barney had broken out.

My favourite memory of Religious Education was the day we drove a supply teacher mental.

Supply teachers were so often the victims of our mischief, unaware of which pupils to look out for, and completely at our mercy when it came to the subject of what we had been working on lately.

'Now, your teacher said we were to cover the Ten Commandments today…'

'Nah, Miss, we've done that'.

'Really?'

'Aye. A couple of times, actually. She told us we were watching *Cool Runnings* today…'

The high point of R.E. came when one supply teacher had the misfortune of teaching us indoors on a very sunny day.

'Please, Miss, can we not go out and play rounders? It's so hot in here'.

'Sorry, guys, your teacher said we had to complete this coursework'.

The heat was near unbearable. The sun shone into the classroom in tantalising shafts of white light. Through the windows we could see freshly cut playing fields and a perfect, unadulterated blue sky. Other classes had been allowed out for kickabouts, races or to do their coursework spread-eagled on the grass.

This was torture.

Slumped on my desk, hard against the wall and next to a window, I stopped writing to strip my jumper off and have a cursory glance at the time. It was only three minutes since I had last looked. The period was dragging in: slower than a week in the jail, and not dissimilar.

I turned my attention back to the jotter in front of me, and in doing so somehow sent a circle of light darting across the classroom. I shot a gaze at the dot on the wall, bemused.

It was the reflection of my watch. The afternoon sunlight streaming into our stuffy classroom was so bright that it was bouncing off my watch face in a perfect, bright circle.

An oh-so-welcome distraction. I grabbed my left-hand wrist and the watch with my other hand, concentrating the aim of the reflection until I had brought it towards my mate Gerry. I landed the circle perfectly on the pages of his jotter.

Confused, he looked up, eyes darting around the classroom until catching sight of me, shining watch and stupid grin. We shared a smile, and Gerry nudged the boy next to him to point out what was going on.

At that, both Gerry and the other boy extended their arms into a shaft of light until it caught the face of their watches. Training their reflections, they aimed their circles at me in retaliation, two white circles dancing around on my delighted face.

Other pupils noticed what was going on, amused. Soon, almost everyone in the class had stopped what they were doing to play with the reflections of their own watch, some twenty odd circles of light now bouncing around the room like some disco ball had fallen from the ceiling and shattered into tiny pieces.

I looked over to see the teacher's reaction but she was oblivious, reading some pulp fiction book that had no relevance to R.E. whatsoever. While we were supposed to be slaving away over some shitey bible pish in sweatshop conditions, she was kicking back with a page-turner? No chance.

I took control of the watch face once more and with my tongue sticking out the side of my mouth in concentration, shone a gleaming circle of light in her eye.

She blinked, recoiled in shock, and looked up in anger.

'What is that?!' she demanded.

Thankfully, before she could pinpoint the timepiece sniper, she had drawn the attention of the class with her outburst. Like a deer staggering unwittingly into the middle of a hunting lodge, her face was almost instantly covered in loads more shimmering dots. Suddenly her face was more sparkly than Elton John's most fabulous sequined jacket.

She tried fruitlessly to look at individual attackers and

plead with them to stop, but each time the blinding glare sent her face this way and that, an arm coming up to protect her face. Shielding behind it, she wailed 'Stop! Stop!'

After one final attempt to look at the class, every pupil's glimmering watch circle dancing around her frowning face, she ran out of the room and was never seen again.

When the year head inevitably came marching in minutes later, we fell silent and took our telling off; but not before one last attack. We were prepared for him, watches at the ready, and no sooner had he burst through the door, full of anger, than his face lit up like the Batsignal in a Gotham emergency.

Just one of life's great theological mysteries: if God exists, why would he allow a classroom full of giggling dickhead teenagers to nearly blind a poor woman with their watch reflections?

I was in so much agony with my stomach that it was no longer a personal, private torment; my mum could tell there was something going on and was ushering the pair of us forward, telling me it would be okay.

We eventually arrived at the house we had seen in the distance, knocked, and were so relieved when the door swung open to reveal a kind, old woman, prepared to listen to our plight and take pity.

'Aw sure that's terrible, come on in now the pair of ye...'

God bless the world-renowned Irish hospitality.

I only just resisted the urge to barge her out of the way in my rush for a bathroom, or the nearest floor space if I couldn't make it that far. I used my very last ounce of restraint (and sphincter strength) to do a John Wayne stroll, bum cheeks clenched, into the living room she ushered us into. We were plied with tea and offered an embarrassment of cakes that even Eamonn Holmes celebrating a Man United treble couldn't clear.

Our situation was soon much better. We had been fed, watered, and help was on its way, following a phone call to our breakdown service. They were a couple of hours away, but our host assured us we could wait it out with her. Things were on the up.

However, my pressing concern was becoming ever more pressing. The call of nature had already called and left several irate voicemail messages. It had to be answered.

I had to go. Now.

X: VIRTUAL INSANITY
'You'll need to pause that, your tea's ready!'

Gamers were spoiled in the 1990s as the two giants of the industry – before Sony or Microsoft had even entered the fray – went head-to-head with their blockbuster consoles: Sega with the Mega Drive and Nintendo with the SNES.

The first great console war produced so many classic titles as the rivals tried to outdo each other: *Super Mario Kart*, *Donkey Kong Country* and *F Zero X* on the SNES, for instance, and games like *Sonic The Hedgehog*, *Earthworm Jim* and *Streets of Rage* on the Sega console.

Nintendo were far stricter with quality control, actually going so far as to impose restrictions on the number of games that third-party publishers could release each year, and reserving the right to reject their work if the company felt it didn't meet their standards.

The makers of the Mega Drive took the opposite tack, boasting a larger library of titles with far greater inconsistency when it came to quality. And it's for that reason that Sega's debut console was the first love of my life.

What separated the Sega console from its competitor

was just how wonderfully odd so many of the games on offer were.

I hate to get all granddad, going wistful and melancholy for the bygone days while sucking on a Werther's Original, but there was a bizarre, nutty quality to games back then that is missing in the current generation of blockbuster games.

Today's best-selling titles are all well and good – whether it's a hyper-realistic war game like *Call of Duty* or *Battlefield*, or a polished sports title like the latest *FIFA* – but how can they possibly compare to our selection of weird games chock full of robots, madcap aliens, outer space adventures and irritating mammals?

For example, one of the most popular titles back then was also one of the strangest, called *Ecco The Dolphin*.

In it, players controlled a bottlenose dolphin named Ecco through a series of ocean levels, some named in tribute to Pink Floyd songs, and on an alien spacecraft as he fought hostile extra-terrestrials.

The only thing crazier than the abstract plot was that the game sold incredibly well despite being complete shite. Even reminiscing now, gamers of my generation don't seem to have forgiven that knobhead dolphin, cursing at the very mention of his name.

The controls were difficult and included such twee and pointless features as the ability to sing, in order to communicate with other cetaceans or interact with objects, a purely aesthetic spin when leaping out of the water, and echolocation, a song which would return to the player in order to generate a map of the surrounding area.

Players would ultimately give up after just a level or two as the difficulty was high and the game unrewarding. No one gave a shit about the stupid dolphin we had been tasked with helping to save and as far as I'm concerned, I hope he never made it to his home planet or wherever the hell he was going. With any luck he got trapped in a plastic bag, the dick.

Another example of the madcap games available to us and arguably weirder still than *Ecco*, *Ballz* was a fighting game in which players could control a roster of characters made completely of balls, including a farting monkey, a caveman, a ballerina and a rhinoceros.

The game proved controversial as it opened with the line, 'To be the champion, you gotta have Ballz!'

Nintendo, always the more conservative of the two console giants, deemed this too lewd for their console, and elected to change the intro to state that '…you gotta play Ballz'.

I'm sure I'm not alone in thinking that that is racier still.

The title's developer, PF Magic, also ran a wonderful ad campaign with the image of a Christmas tree made of balls, and the immortal caption, 'Tell your mom you want Ballz for Christmas'.

Yeah, so I will.

Other crazy and off-the-wall games included *Bubsy* (about a cat whose collection of yarn balls has been stolen by a race of fabric-stealing aliens called 'Woolies'), *James Pond* (an underwater 007 spoof featuring a suave, suit-wearing fish as the titular character) and *Worms* (worms going to battle with insane weapons such as grenades and flamethrowers).

Even something as seemingly straightforward as a cash-in on *The Simpsons* was done in the weirdest way possible, firstly with *Bart Simpson vs. The Space Mutants* (in which you play Bart, the only Springfield resident aware of an alien attack, spray-painting objects purple and destroying hats in order to save the town) and later in *The Simpsons: Bart's Nightmare* (where the aim is to guide Bart through a bad dream in which he is a dinosaur, the superhero Bartman, and ends up trapped in his own blood stream).

So many of the weird and wonderful games on offer could only belong to the 1990s. It's impossible to think of any developer hitting out with such nutty ideas in the modern day. Take for example the glorious slice of nineties' video gaming that was *Moonwalker*, a Michael Jackson vehicle released on the Sega Mega Drive.

As if to solidify its nineties' credentials, it features genius, synthesised 16-bit versions of Jacko's biggest hits throughout. In fact, it has everything you could possibly want from a Michael Jackson themed game: Bubbles the monkey, dance moves and plenty of 'Ow!' noises.

Better yet, the plot involves Jackson battling through level after level in order to collect children.

Yes, to collect children. That's right, the entertainer who twice appeared in court to clear his name of child sex offences licensed a game in which players took control of him in order to round up kidnapped youngsters and rescue them.

'Hey kids, I'll save you – jump in the van! Chamon!'

As management missteps go, whoever advised him on that one had a real howler. What else was considered at the games development meeting where that title was conceived? An OJ Simpson licensed racing sim where players flee from pursuing police? The 18-rated *Mike Tyson: Date Night*? Or perhaps *Kerb Crawling with Hugh Grant*?

The early days of the console war saw loads of mad shite being licensed, all of it sitting perfectly at home amongst the scattergun, schizophrenic catalogue of the Mega Drive – everything from *McDonald's Treasure Land Adventure* to *Cool Spot*, a game based on the logo from the 7UP adverts, right through to a totally fucking mental *Home Improvement* game featuring aliens, dinosaurs and dragons. Yes, *Home Improvement*, as in the Tim Allen sitcom about a TV personality handyman. And yes, aliens, dinosaurs and dragons.

While games were plainly crazier then, they were also more inherently entertaining. As well as being a lot less adventurous in terms of plot and ideas, today's games are so lifelike as to lose some of the silly fun that was to be had in playing something that was quite clearly a fictional game and an escape from reality.

Modern football titles such as the latest *Pro Evo* or *FIFA* might look photorealistic and offer a level of control previously unparalleled, but do they provide players with the same joy that classic games such as *World Cup Italia '90*, *Sensible Soccer* or *FIFA International Soccer* offered?

Having referees who provide realism by 'playing advantage' and waiting until the ball next goes out of play to book players is all very well, but wasn't playing with your mate more fun when there were simply no fouls at all, as in *World Cup Italia '90*?

There was only one form of tackle in *WCI90* and that was a crazy, red-eyed, puffed-chest, Roy Keane type snap which was always deemed A-OK in the eyes of the officials. You flew in to every crunching challenge as gracefully as an Eric Cantona kung-fu kick, leaving the player lying in a mangled heap, sticking his hand down his shorts to rearrange his testicles.

Modern soccer games and their facial capture technology might depict players so accurately that your granddad will naively ask 'What match is that you're watching?', but who can help but look back with fondness on the days when *ISS Pro* didn't even have the license for players' names? Your team would boast such legends of the field as Robbie Fooler, Steve McMananan and Paul Gascone. Heroes, every one, with about as much resemblance to their real-life counterparts as a potato with a smiley face drawn on in marker pen.

In 1994, we were blessed with two of the greatest football titles of all time: *FIFA International Soccer* and *World Cup USA '94*. Gamers of a certain age would sooner play these two games than just about any other football release.

FIFA International Soccer still plays magnificently well to this day, and while it might have been bested in every possible technical aspect by its modern descendants, it can rival any current football title on the most important criterion of all: the sheer fun to be had while playing it.

Many a childhood Saturday was spent fighting out epic Germany v Brazil matches with pals, always trying to get your player into that sneaky position from which you could shoot for a guaranteed goal. Players could avoid being booked by the referee for as long as they were prepared to run away from him, and goals could be scored by getting in front of the opposition goalie as he was taking a punt - a guaranteed way to piss off your mate.

World Cup USA '94 was similarly brilliant, although not without its problems: it was almost impossible to launch a game, thanks to America's poor choice of World Cup mascot.

Let me explain.

That year's World Cup was hosted in America. The USA's ingenious idea for a World Cup mascot was, for reasons unknown, the international symbol of global football that is the cartoon dog. It was, at least, wearing a football kit.

This is the world's biggest sporting event. It's special; it only rolls round once every four years. Billions glued to their screens, pride and glory at stake for every competing nation. Yet you would have been forgiven for thinking that the American organising committee behind this dog-led campaign were hosting a small-time Crufts-style event. Rather than the pinnacle of one of the most popular sports in the world, anyone seeing the canine-themed advertising materials was put in mind of some village fete, with the opportunity to buy some jam, throw a few wet sponges at the local vicar and cheer throughout the main event as some cute dogs chased around a soft football for the amusement of onlooking kids.

Striker The Dog was an awful choice of mascot and even worse as a means of navigating a video game menu.

Yes, *World Cup USA '94* was almost unplayable thanks to Striker's presence in the options screens. Where any normal football game would have menu options written in text - like 'Single player', 'Two player' and '5-minute game' or '10-minute game' - *USA '94* took the bizarre step of representing these options only with pictures of this idiot of a dog in a variety of cryptic stances.

Children had to confusingly navigate their way around such pictures as Dog, Two Dogs, Dog With Whistle, Dog With Offside Flag, Dog Standing Next To A Television or Dog Tying His Shoelace until eventually finding themselves at kick-off.

Spare a thought for those who never did and were just endlessly lost in menu after menu of dogs striking increasingly stupid stances.

So we've established so far that games in the 1990s were nuttier, braver, more fun and a bit more pedophile-y (thanks, *Moonwalker*).

I would also argue that many of the games were harder than anything on the market now.

Video games then were ridiculously difficult, made more difficult still with the lack of a save feature. Some games had a password system that let you automatically jump to certain levels but for the most part if you wanted to complete a game, you did it in one stressful sitting, wrestling with it for months to perfect near-impossible challenges.

Case in point, *Back to the Future Part III*. This movie tie-in featured a mere FOUR levels but had young gamers cursing the very day they were born. If only they had been drowned in a sack at birth like an unwanted litter of cats, they wouldn't have had to suffer the torment of wrestling with this horrible, relentlessly difficult game.

The first level pitted you against an obstacle-laden desert with a series of gunfights and jumps as you fought to stop Clara Clayton and her runaway horse from falling into a ravine. The only possible way of clearing this opening challenge was to literally memorise every gunshot, every jump and every duck of the head, to play through so many times that you could completely rely on muscle memory to get you over the line. By the time you did, days or weeks of practice had gone into getting there and it felt like the end credit screen should be your reward; yet that was merely the first hurdle cleared, thumbprints replaced with blistered and withered skin like couch leather.

The second level, while difficult by any other standards, was the easiest of the four tasks. It involved a shooting gallery at a county fair, hitting a series of pop-up ducks and avoiding civilians. It was another that involved a lot of practice, but unlike the first level it wasn't so stupidly tough that you had to trade parts of your soul for the sake of its completion.

The third level involved, of all things, a pie fight. Enemies appeared from saloon doors and windows, while you were tasked with killing them all with a lethal pie Frisbee. Bizarre, but eventually doable, if you were prepared to surrender all of your summer holidays and dedicate every waking minute to perfecting the art of clearing it. By the time you had bettered level three, you had lost whatever was left of your childhood and probably some of your sight along with it.

Level four was the most difficult yet. Players had to battle their way along the top of a moving steam train, dodging puffs of smoke and enemies, collecting fuel along the way and eventually navigating the hardest part of the whole game.

Just when you thought the end was in sight, the toughest challenge reared its ugly head. At the very end of the last level, the developers tasked you with clearing a gauntlet of steam bursts. The final carriage had a line of vents out of which erupted jets of steam, seemingly at random. Your fingers would be shaking, months of practice coming down to this one obstacle, and you would inevitably make a mistake and lose your last life just before the very end.

Other horrible challenges gamers still have nightmares

about include:

- Flying through the lava level on your magic carpet in *Disney's Aladdin*.

- *Sonic The Hedgehog* and the final climb of 'Labyrinth Zone Act 3' in rising water, with the panic-inducing music if you started to run out of breath, and subsequent boss fight.

- The water temple in *Legend of Zelda: Ocarina of Time*. The fucking water bastard of a temple in Legend of pissing Zelda and her stupid Ocarina of FUCK.

- The last level of *Streets of Rage*, where players had to re-do every previous boss fight and then defeat the endboss, Mr. X.

Another key difference between gaming then and now is that in the Mega Drive era of the early 1990s, kids were given carte blanche to buy and play whatever video games they bloody well pleased. *Call of Duty*, *Grand Theft Auto V*, *Battlefield 4*, *Gears of War*; just some of the most popular, modern-day video games to be given an '18' age rating.

Our games? Not an age rating in sight.

Streets of Rage. A relentless, all-action 'beat 'em up' in which you control one of three ex-police officers fighting a crime syndicate which has brought violence and death to their once-peaceful city. Through level after level, the player is besieged by seemingly endless waves of savage thugs whose only desire is to maim, stab or kill you. The ex-cops must fight them off with punches, kicks, an array of weapons that include knives, broken bottles, lead pipes and baseball bats, and even the assistance of friends in the force who can rain down explosive rounds of machine-gun fire. No age rating.

Golden Axe. Players battle through a medieval-style fantasy world in order to retrieve the magical emblem of their land, the eponymous axe. The three playable characters, Gilius, Ax and Tyris wield a battle axe, two-handed broadsword and a longsword respectively. These warriors fight to the death with soldiers, knights and skeletons armed with clubs and maces whose only desire is, again, to maim, stab or kill you. No age rating.

Doom. A first-person shooter (some would say THE first-person shooter) in which you play through the eyes of the only marine left on Mars to fight throngs of monsters and prevent an attack on Earth, armed with only a pistol. Throughout the game, weapons upgrades include chainsaws, shotguns, rocket launchers and plasma rifles. After contending with demon hordes, toxic slime pits and fireball attacks, eventually fighting your way through Hell, your soldier arrives back on Earth to find that while he survived scores of murderous beasts and their attempts to maim, stab and kill, his efforts have all been in vein and the demons have wrought chaos and destruction upon Earth. No age rating.

Then along came the game that changed it all. Before the *Grand Theft Auto* series with its prostitute murders and witness torture, even before *Modern Warfare 2* with its infamous airport shooting spree scene, there was the original; the first game that ever had parents and politicians wringing their hands and praying to the skies, asking the Lord where we as a society went wrong and begging for redemption.

Before this controversial work of the Devil, I and many other kid gamers of the 1990s could walk into any games retailer on the high street and purchase cartridges with impunity. Not any more. This bad boy was the first game I ever owned which came with an age rating emblazoned on the front, as an appeal to decent human beings everywhere, a warning that only the bravest and most twisted individuals should dare to even open the box.

That game was *Disney's The Lion King*. Given all that had gone before it, imagine just how tasteless and controversial *The Lion King* must have been that ratings councils convened and felt that this, finally, was the game on which they had to slap a warning label on the cover.

This was the first video game in my extensive collection which had been deemed too depraved for kids of a certain age. With a '3+' label on the box, parents were plainly warned that only kids over the age of three should even think about inserting this pile of filth into their cartridge slot.

Of course, it went without saying that tots of any age could be left alone to play as vigilantes taking the law into their own hands to bludgeon criminals to death on the streets, as barbarians in nothing but their pants chopping skeleton warriors to pieces, and as a marooned soldier firing round after round into undead armies.

However, no one was willing to find out what would happen if we exposed those same tots to a lion cub who could roar, roll and bounce, all whilst collecting bugs in the colourful kingdom from the popular Disney film of the same name.

It was a push-too-far of the envelope. Which sick, depraved individuals had created this disgraceful affront to all that was good and proper?

Of course, video games age ratings had actually been brought in to combat a wave of controversial titles such as *Lethal Enforcers*, *Night Trap* and *Mortal Kombat*, but the reality is that the first time most kids came across an age rating was with something as innocent as Simba and his 'Hakuna Matata' outlook on life.

Give me an unrated, unrealistic, unhinged Mega Drive game over any of the current crop of video games, every time.

Today's gamers may think they have it made, with their online multiplayers, DLC, voice-operated consoles and movement-controlled games, but you haven't truly lived until you've had to blow on the cartridge half a dozen times before seeing that singsong 'SE-GA!' screen flash up, then pray you don't once again lose the last life of your last 'Continue' on that last bloody boss fight...

XI: ALL MY BEST FRIENDS ARE METALHEADS
'A/S/L?'

Children of our generation and earlier would have been amazed to learn that the future would bring devices – some pocket-sized – with which people could remotely access all human knowledge at the click of a button. They would have been more astonished still to learn that most of us would only use the Internet to look at stupid pictures of cats and argue with strangers about exactly when *The Simpsons* went into decline.

No longer for us, Teletext and its one-paragraph Saturday night football summaries, or twenty-page cinema listings which would invariably start at the page just after the one you wanted, meaning a ten minute wait for a too-short glance at the information required.

No, now we have the Internet, a creation that has proven to be at turns ghastly and fantastic.

Personally, the World Wide Web has resulted in few greater outcomes than the time in my teens that I came across a young Irish chap of the same age as I, browsing and posting on a heavy metal message board I frequented, who went by the online handle of 'Colossal Poo'.

I knew Peter McCaughan was a potential friend based solely on his magnificent username. That feeling was compounded by his hilariously funny message board posts, littered with sexy tales, outrageous stories and, of course, toilet humour.

In even a small sample, one can get a measure of this fine fellow's fantastic character:

- My name is Peter McCaughan and I just followed through.

- I thought this was going to be where we could all list a 'whatever happened to...'
Whatever happened to Vipers? You used to always hear about them - like, remote control cars would be called SUPER VIPER, or a fictional team in a cartoon soccer series might be called THE VIPERS.
What ever happened to Vipers?

- 37% of me is made entirely out of bees.

- My mum said she'd, very generously, give me £50 for new shoes... so I got £6 Gola council estate specials from Dunnes, then spent the rest on games and booze.

- I had to wipe my ass with cheap tissues the other day (not toilet roll, tissues).... and before I spotted the tissues it was very, very, very nearly panty liners.
Imagine that... a fanny pad up your arse, yowza!

- My friend says that he'd rather have the semen of six men rubbed all over his face than eat their pubes. I think that is just obscene.

- Last night my friend said he 'saw something on the news' about a really big burger... after a bit of cajoling he admitted it was actually 'Newsround'

- I finally fixed my Mega Drive, and popped in 'Micro Machines '96'...

You may remember that this game features a track editor, so you can design your own courses and race on them?

Well, I thought I'd give it a bash... and made an outdoor course, with a ramp, a winding sorta feel, megafast cars and had it marked out with peas and other foodstuffs, like to show the edge of the 'road'.

I called this track, 'POOWWERLD'

Then I went to save it... I nearly bust a gut laughing when it transpired that, when I had last played this game/used the track editor (I was probably about 12), I had also created a track called 'POOWORLD'. I booted the track up and lo and behold, it was very, very, very, very nearly identical, save for a few extra twists and turns.

I guess some things never change.

- One night when I was 15 I arrived home wearing only a purple thong and a pair of hobnail boots... from what I hear a policeman had to remove me from a tree.

- I went into a toilet cubicle the other day, after a few pints, with a pen in one hand and my cock in the other (well I didn't get my cock out 'til I got inside the toilet... for once)

My intention was to write 'JOHN CANDY' on the wall, in big letters.

I didn't tell a SOUL about this plan.

Lo and behold, some cunt beat me to it.

What are the odds of THAT?!

- One time my friend wet the bed when he was about 13...

His mum asked if he'd had a wet dream.

What the fuck kind of BEAST does she think he is?!

- Once I went on holiday to York with my folks... they went and did the touristy things during the day, looked at a wall and stuff.... we split up after breakfast and met at dinner.

They said 'So Pete, what all did you do today?'

'I went to Pizza Hut buffet.'
'Oh! And then what?'
'Uh... and then I met you...'
I was there ALL day, was GREAT! Had to poo in the middle, was scared in case they'd take my plate thinking I was gone. Wiped extra fast.

It was like being back in school and wanting to make friends with the cool kid. I so badly wanted to down a beer or ten with this bearded rascal I knew only as Colossal Poo.

We started an online friendship, chatting on MSN Messenger about Sega Mega Drive games and comics and old horror films and such like. When I heard about *Second Life* – a game in which players control avatars in an online virtual world – he was naturally the first person I thought to approach about going on to troll the life out of it.

A small gang of us downloaded the game, made our own avatars and wasted away nights heckling nerds, in itself a pretty nerdy thing to do. The vast majority of Residents, as players are known, take their *Second Life* very seriously. We did not. Peter and I got thrown out of virtual bars, virtual casinos, virtual house parties, virtual weddings, almost always for sporting boners while wearing nothing but a smile.

The avatars could do everything imaginable – including all the toilet and sexual functions an immature guy could ask for – so online meet after online meet got hijacked by us, with a spot of defecation here, a bit of wanking there and more than one pee party. There was bad language, there was harassment, there was a pink thong. It was fantastic.

The longer I knew Peter, the wilder my impression of him was. He seemed to have no end of crazy stories, always regaling us with tales of his countless mad adventures. I began to hope that he was everything he had painted himself to be online, and wasn't just a boring impostor hiding behind his keyboard persona.

When I finally got the chance to meet him for the first time, it was to head off to an independent rock and metal music festival in Northern Ireland together. Instead, we ended up meeting up with his mate Tierney, going out to sea and spending a full afternoon drinking cider in his boat.

The second time we hooked up, our afternoon was spent in a Mongolian restaurant in the heart of Glasgow, eating zebra, kangaroo, springbok, crocodile and wild boar, with a spicy sauce called 'Boaby's Bum Buster' and Haggisbombs (Jägermeister and Irn-Bru) to wash it all down. We pretended it was his birthday for the right to sit on the special occasion throne and don Mongolian warrior robes, then had a swordfight in the middle of the restaurant.

The third time just involved alcohol.

Peter was everything I had hoped he would be.

As I reminisced more and more about my own childhood, and pondered just how freakishly similar the childhoods of so many of my Scottish pals had been, I began to wonder which phenomenon had made it across the pond. Here was a guy with a similar sense of humour, of a similar age, with a similar taste in everything from retro video games to comic books. Our adulthood had followed such similar paths: we both loved heavy metal, cider boat times, Mongolian swordfights and heckling nerds. It stood to reason that his childhood must have been alike as well.

Had he also bought cap gun refills from the ice cream van and terrified his own neighbourhood? Did the yo-yo craze of the late '90s hit Northern Ireland too? Did pupils at his school get their trousers whipped down, and was the practice known as 'skegging' over there, or did they call it something different? I had to find out, so sat down with the great man to pick his silly, fucked-up brain.

I have a theory that as well as a 'dog in school day', every school has a 'Phantom Shitter'; a mysterious pupil who randomly poos in unexpected places such as urinals, sinks or even corridors. Any stories which help verify this?

I absolutely do, man. We most certainly did have a Phantom Shitter.

I remember it really well; it was one of the best days in school. I was sitting in R.E., Religious Education, and a guy literally burst into the room and said 'Oh my god, someone's done a shite on the floor of the toilet!'

They had done a shit on the floor and obviously I ran pretty much straight out to go and look at it. The whole day was magical: people bringing their friends in, even girls just going 'Look at that!'

It was just amazing.

You actually ran out of class to go check it out?

Yeah, pretty much. It was one of those days where, you know, it was a substitute teacher or something where it wasn't a *real* class, so it was definitely okay. But I think even if it hadn't have been that kinda class, I would have run out. It's not every day that somebody does an honest-to-god shit on the floor.

What you might be interested in is that I heard of some new developments on this. A family member is a teacher in a school and they were telling me that they have a real ongoing problem at the minute with something called 'hot-dogging', where these guys are getting hot dog buns from the canteen and doing shites in them and leaving them all round the school!

Like they'll be turning up on top of door frames so that somebody opens the door. It's kind of like the old *Beano* water bucket thing but it's a hot dog bun with a shite on it!

So I really like that there's been real progress. For me, I

thought it had reached its logical conclusion, but it seems like there's miles to go. We're standing on the shoulders of giants, man.

It's a wee bit like Heelys all over again. I don't know if you've seen these little shoes that kids have now, they've got wheels on the bottom. They can just skate through supermarkets and down corridors. I look at them and go: 'Why the fuck did we not have them when we were kids?!'
It's like that all over again.

Totally. It's the Heelys of shites.

I have a fairly awful story later in the book that involves my first camping trip as a teen, where my mate got, shall we say, 'caught short'. Alcohol was involved. I seem to remember you have a very similar, no less horrific tale... What happened?

I totally do. I think it was just after school. Me and a lifelong pal, Aiden, and my heterosexual life mate, Tierney, were going on a camping trip.

Our friend Aiden rang us up, he said: 'Dudes, there's this seafood festival on, in the wilds of Donegal.'

I was like, 'Seafood festival? I dunno'.

'Listen, it's really good, there's a bit of seafood, but it's mostly just all these ridiculous bastards coming from far and wide to get pissed'.

'Alright man, fuck it, why not? But where are we gonna stay?'

And he says: 'Well, I've got a friend whose parents own a holiday home down there, and my mate says that it'll be fine for us to camp in the garden'.

'Alright, fair enough, no problem' - I didn't question why that was such a weird thing, but nonetheless we headed down. It's a four or five hour drive, and we're about twenty minutes away from this tiny village. It's like a one horse town, there's a bar and a chip shop and that's it.

Pretty much everything you need.

Totally, there's literally nothing else I would need.

So Aiden says: 'Listen, dudes, I gotta level with you. I couldn't get my mate on the phone. He doesn't know we're gonna be staying in the garden. But it'll be fine'.

We were kind of pissed at him, but I was also kinda pissed, cos I'd been drinking whisky out of the bottle the whole way down. It made it seem a bit funnier but nonetheless, we were a bit perturbed. We weren't about to turn back or anything, so we go into this village, we get into this guy's house.

He lives in a beach-side cottage sort of thing, it's on this lovely sloping road, lovely, gorgeous, rural Donegal. Just going down to this beautiful ocean. A lovely view. He's got these steps going down to a back garden.

We go into the back garden, we set up our tents and stuff. It's pissing down raining, really badly. So me, Aiden and Tierney are all sitting in my tent, just having a couple of beers. We had bought loads of funny fake noses for the journey so we're messing around with these fake noses, Aiden put one of them on his dick.

But Tierney says he needs to do a shit.

So I says 'Man, look, it's a tiny village, the bar is right there' – it's like maybe a fifty second jog at most.

He says he can't make it.

'Oh, I dunno, man', I said. 'We're in this guy's back garden - do you wanna do a shit in a bush or something?'

'No, no, no - if I do that you'll take a photograph of me'.

Of course I said 'There's no way I'll take a photograph of you'.

I *obviously* would have taken a photograph of him.

So he concocts this amazing idea where he can run up

the back steps, back to this guy's front garden, run straight down to the beach and do a shite behind the sand dune - thinking it'll take him a maximum of twenty-five to thirty seconds. Probably his timing was about right.

As he's running up the back steps, thumping his feet on the ground, me and Aiden hear a car pulling into the driveway. At which point, being the good friends that we are, we started shouting after him, going: 'Tierney, somebody's coming here' - maybe turn back so we can explain why we're in this fucker's garden!

It's obviously way too late. Tierney has not only made the driveway at the same time that this guy arrives at his house, but he's caught short, has pulled down his trousers and is doing this horrible shite all over this man's driveway.

I saw the shite later on, it was disgusting. It was bright orange. It was like the worst thing a dog would do, a kind of Irn-Bru colour. Just horrible.

So what happens, as he's doing this shite everywhere, this guy pulls up in a BMW, which I think - I dunno, there was some talk of it maybe being nicked or something!

He's doing this shite, the guy arrives, this nut job, by the way - the year before, apparently, he had got arrested for taking all of his clothes off and not putting them back on. His dad had to come and get him out of jail, all this ridiculous shit.

This guy arrives, Tierney's shitting everywhere, he pulls up his trousers really quickly, just as the guy drives in. So the guy hasn't seen any arse action, per se. The guy gets out of the car, and for all intents and purposes sees this weird fucker just standing in his driveway, looking really shifty.

He says: 'Sorry mate, can I help you at all?'

And Tierney starts talking really fast, saying 'Oh, listen, I'm friends with your mate Aiden, I met you before actually one time, uh, he, he said we could stay in your garden' - and he's freaking out and all.

And the guy just says: 'Whoa, slow down a second –

you're staying in my garden?!'

Meanwhile, Tierney has been flanked by this guy's girlfriend – who's from a particularly rough area of west Belfast - and she sees exactly what he's done on the ground.

She just screams: 'Oh my god, he's done a fucking shite!'

By this point, me and Aiden have crept up the steps a bit and are watching from here on.

Tierney starts bracing himself for a punch in the face, but the guy looks at Tierney and looks at the shite and goes, 'Tell you what, mate, it happens to everyone! Sure, come on, get your pals and we'll have a drink in the house!'

Now, *obviously*, it doesn't happen to everyone - but this guy's such a lunatic that he didn't mind Tierney shiteing all over the driveway. So you know, it's a very happy ending - about as happy as it could be.

Tierney came and got us, we went in the house and we stayed all weekend, it was a good time!

There were loads more terrible things happened that weekend - a guy cut his toe off jumping off the back of a speedboat because he was 'trying to do a Baywatch'. But in terms of the actual shiteing, it went as well as humanly possible!

The 1990s seemed to be the era of the toy comeback: the Rubik's Cube reappeared briefly, Pogs came back into fashion in a big way and marbles even had a wee turn of being cool again in our school. But the king of all these revitalised toys was the yo-yo. In the late 1990s, you were absolutely nothing unless you could bust a few moves and pull off a couple of tricks with your yo-yo. Ours improved upon those of previous generations; with a ball bearing mechanism inside, the new yo-yo could be flicked down into a long-lasting spin, giving the user time to show off some tricks.

You once told me about you going off on some mad yo-yo related adventure. What was the deal with that?

I was in first year, first form, so aged eleven or twelve or whatever it was. I had gone to London - my folks had taken me away on a lovely family holiday, it was amazing - and this was at the height of the yo-yo craze. I think it was the first iteration of it, it came and went a bit, but this was its real zenith.

I don't know if you remember him endorsing yo-yos, but this man from Phoenix, Arizona, Yo Hans - the yo-yo king - was in Hamley's, the toy shop.

So I was like, 'Aw, we gotta go to Hamley's! We gotta see Yo Hans!'

I took part in this yo-yo contest that he's running and I don't think I won it, I think I came second or third. But it was cool. To a yo-yo obsessed twelve year old, it was cool.

My folks were really nice and they bought me this amazing yo-yo called the Turbo Bumblebee, which was just the pièce de résistance of yo-yos. At the time it was sixty quid, which is fucking nuts, for a yo-yo! I've still got it.

So we do this competition and it's amazing. I'm over the moon about this. It's like meeting a hero of mine, I'm delighted.

The rest of the holiday is amazing, I'm playing with this yo-yo and all this stuff, it's real cool.

Then we get back to sunny Belfast – this, I guess, was the start of the summer holidays, so start of July or something – we get back to Newtownards, just outside Belfast, where I'm from.

Towards the end of the holidays, we get the news that Yo Hans is coming to do a yo-yo show in this shopping centre in Bangor.

I went: 'Oh my god, I gotta see this guy again!'

Not in like a gay way or anything!

...I dunno, maybe in a bit of a gay way?

I'm picturing by this point you've got posters in the bedroom and stuff...

Totally, man. He gave me a poster later on. I've got loads of these yo-yos. I've got the amazing one my parents gave me, but I've got loads more - like thirty or forty yo-yos, bought from all over the world. I'm fucking obsessed.

So he comes and he does this show and afterwards I go: 'I actually saw you a couple of months back in London, and it was amazing'.

He says 'Oh man, yeah, totally, the yo-yo kid! I remember you!'

And everyone's the fucking yo-yo kid I'm sure, but he was really nice.

I don't even know how this happened, but he must have heard that I was good, or remembered it.

So he says: 'Listen, I'm going on a tour. Of shopping centres' - it was around a real shitty, maybe, twenty mile radius - 'Do you wanna come with me?'

Which I did! I thought I was 'the bomb', just going round these shitty shops like Woolworths, doing some tricks with Yo Hans, being his right hand man. The ballboy of yo-yos.

I remember a couple of wee guys asked me for my autograph, which is just ludicrous.

But the highlight of it was when we went for a pub lunch and he taught me some techniques for breaking into cars. He was telling me how if you cut a tennis ball in half and you put it over the lock of a car and pop it, it pops the lock up.

I never tried it, I dunno, but I guess if I ever really need to get into a shitty old Clio or something, Yo Hans may have helped me out.

Sounds like you probably learned more in the

summer holidays than you did in school that year.

Dude, that was my 'Wonder Years'! Although when I got back to school, there was a thing about it in the local paper, of me and Yo Hans – I'm doing some fun shit like making a star or something – and I thought, 'Aw yeah, everyone's going to think that's so cool!'

They didn't. There was one particular guy – who I'm friends with now – every time I saw him he was all 'Yo-yo wanker!'

And quite rightly too!

Did you have an outfit that you had to wear?

I didn't have a special outfit, but I remember that Yo Hans had a backwards Kangol cap, so I wore one of those too, just because I wanted to try and be cool.

Also, he used a billiards glove – like a gossamer glove, the stuff that tights are made out of but black – but he had the index and middle fingers cut off, and the other two covered by the glove. I can't really remember why - but I remember he made me a couple of these, so I still have these black half-gloves that he gave me! And probably a Kangol cap somewhere too.

So yeah, it wasn't an outfit, but it was kind of a costume.

I'm picturing it like the episode of *The Simpsons*, where the guys come to do the yo-yo tricks in their school and then pile into the back of a crappy old van.

Dude, it was exactly like that. It was pretty much exactly like that. I imagine he's probably folded up somewhere in the back of a Scooby Doo van right now, ready to be dusted off for the next craze. He's hanging out with Pog Man somewhere.

Everyone thinks their decade or their era had the best of everything: film, music, football, whatever is up for debate, people of all generations insist that it was never better than when they were a lad. But truly, the end of the '90s was THE time to be a wrestling fan. Fresh from legends like Macho Man Randy Savage, Hulk Hogan, Jake The Snake Roberts, Bret The Hitman Hart and Roddy Piper, we were absolutely spoiled with even better characters: The Rock and his arch nemesis Triple H, Stone Cold Steve Austin, the fantastically bizarre Mick Foley, The Big Show, The Undertaker. There were new matches like Hell In A Cell, Tables Ladders and Chairs, and Buried Alive. Great times.

As young secondary school lads, our trousers were permanently covered in grass stain marks from rolling about in Suplexes, Powerbombs and DDTs. The lunchtime Royal Rumble was just a summer tradition. Any similar defiance of the 'Don't try this at home' warning over your way? I would literally put my house on you having some cracking wrestling anecdotes.

It wasn't really a wrestling mishap, but it was pretty late in school – I guess it was the last year in school – I went to see Fozzy, wrestler Chris Jericho's metal band, which was just ludicrous. At the time I had taken to kind of dressing as a cowboy. So I had these dungarees on, these knee-high cowboy boots, a Stetson.

Obviously this kind of gig, it was fifty-fifty metal fans and wrestling fans, and there's some Venn diagram overlap there. There were these dudes there from one of the local backyard wrestling federations and they were showing me pictures of them with barbed wire and all, jumping off their houses onto each other's faces and stuff.

And they were like: 'Oh man, we love your cowboy shtick. Do you wanna be a backyard wrestler?'

I got so drunk, I was like: 'Totally! Totally, I could

totally be a wrestler! I'd be an amazing wrestler!'

I forgot all about it until a week later, they phoned me up and said 'Man, we're waiting'.

They were waiting in some guy's house for me!

I didn't go though, I had to say 'Listen, I'm really sorry, I don't want to be a wrestler. I'd like my face to be intact.'

I never really had any major wrestling or childhood mishaps; there were lots of wrestling, garden fun times, but it never went badly wrong.

I think that's the one time I narrowly avoided, you know, a real serious wrestling injury.

Narrowly avoided accidentally becoming a wrestler.

Yes. I guess I could probably say technically for about three hours, I was probably technically a wrestler. But I didn't wrestle at any point during it.

I did wrestle one guy in a toilet. There was a guy who dressed as Triple H and then took off all his clothes except for this ridiculous, tiny banana hammock thing and I think we had a wrestle in the toilet. It's not meant to sound as gay as it does. I think that was my only wrestling match and I'm going to say that I won it. He got thrown out, so...

Reminiscing about childhood over the years, I've always taken great pleasure in finding how universal some games and stories are. Everyone played 'Kerby' and everyone played 'Chappy', just as everyone knew a wooded path where you could be certain of finding discarded porno, or had a teacher who would come in hungover.

So in that spirit, I'm certain that you must have had a 'Jay' in your group of chums. That is, a chap like Jay from *The Inbetweeners*: a liar who everyone else tolerated for reasons no one could quite say. A lad

who would make weird and wonderful, totally unsubstantiated claims.

Ours, Alistair, claimed to be sexually active (promiscuous, even) at a worryingly early age, had any game or album long before anyone else (he got *Pokemon Red* and *Blue* 'from America' and claimed to have a copy of Slipknot's rarer-than-hen's-teeth *Mate. Feed. Kill. Repeat.* debut) and could beat your boldest claim where anything was concerned; just without any actual proof.

Who was your Jay, what lies did he tell and what utter nonsense did he try his best to fool you with?

There were quite a few.

There's Ryan Lennon – I'm trying to remember the ins and outs of that but I think he said he was the world's best player at *Goldeneye 007*, basically.

There were other people who had probably better remain nameless. One such one was this guy who claimed he had been out on a night in Dublin with Colin Farrell, and Colin Farrell had dropped his little black book of babes! This guy had got it, taken it home and phoned all these girls and got off with them. The plot holes in that are so many!

I don't know why Colin Farrell would actually carry around a book of numbers of these magical babes he would call. If this guy then did get a hold of this, if he called them, what was he going to say?

(*Does an impression of Colin Farrell on the phone*) 'Aw Jesus, I'm Colin Farrell…'

And then if he did meet up with them, they would quickly realise he wasn't Colin Farrell. But I think he was trying to say that he would hook up with them and they would just be so impressed that he knew Colin Farrell well enough to use his book, or some weird shit. But that was, obviously, totally bullshit.

There's so many, many more. There was a guy who

swore blind that Megadeth were called Megadeth because Dave Mustaine had actually killed three people, and that he had seen about it in the news!

This same guy, also, a bunch of us told him that there was an early, rare Smashing Pumpkins release that came in a clock and to get the CD out you had to take the clock apart. This guy was all like, 'Yeah, I've got the clock'.

He kept saying he was going to bring it into school, but he didn't bring the clock in, because, well, obviously the clock doesn't exist. I still think he might even still believe that one.

He also said that he played bass on stage with The Smiths at one point as well. That's a guy called Shipman.

Pretty much all these guys got caught out by doing that lie at school and then: 'Well, bring it into school then'.

'Um, yep, I'll ehh, bring it in. My pal's got it just now, I'll get it back off him…'

My favourite thing to do in school was, I liked to subvert it and – it's not quite telling a lie. I liked to start rumours and then try as an adult to maintain them.

We started a rumour, successfully, that our friend Sean, in third year, shit himself. Me and a few mates made it up – we started talking about it I guess in sixth year at school, we started saying: 'Oh, do you remember when Sean shit himself that time?'

And people would say: 'No, I don't remember him shitting himself…'

We'd say, 'No, no, he had to go round the home ec. department and get a towel to clean himself up, and they got him a spare pair of shorts and stuff'.

And then people would say: 'Aw yeah, yeah he did shit himself!'

We did it so much that now, even as a grown man, if I see him I'll bring it up around friends and he'll go 'I never shit myself! I never shit myself!'

But everyone believes that he did. So that was a lying experiment that I personally liked to do.

Slightly more ludicrously I also started a rumour towards the end of school that Tierney – again, the driveway man – had gone to do a reading in assembly but unbeknownst to him a queen spider had gotten into his arse a week before, laid loads of eggs and the eggs all hatched out in his arse - and he had these spiders crawling around his trouser leg, all over the stage at assembly. And that was one people genuinely believed happened.

People say 'I saw that happen!', even though, of course, it never – how could that ever happen?!

But I meet people from school and they say 'Jesus, do you remember the time all those spiders came out of Tierney's arse?!'

I think if that happened, Tierney would probably remember that.

There was a while where he almost seemed to believe it himself. But no, of course it never happened. Maybe I was the liar, that's the problem here - I was the Jay of our group. Shit, that's a horrible thought.

It feels a little dirty to admit this, but I had both a Mega Drive and a SNES as a nipper. Kids then were fairly strict about the fact that you had to be one or the other - a Sega man or a Nintendo man, but never both. Deep down I suppose my heart belonged to the former.

So, which were you? And what are your fondest memories of gaming at a young age? Any favourite games?

Dude, totally the Mega Drive, hands down. Still would be. I mean, I still have a bunch of Mega Drives. At one point I had a Mega Drive in the bathroom, that's how much of a Mega Drive obsessive I am. I was, and still am.

Backup Mega Drives.

Backup Mega Drives, totally. I still play *Sonic The Hedgehog 2* on my phone every time I do a shit. So I guess that's your next answer: *Sonic The Hedgehog 2* was huge for me. It was just amazing when it came out. It was blindingly fast which was like something I had never seen before.

The music was so good. The music to 'Chemical Plant Zone 2' is my favourite game music of all time. As a wee guy – I don't know if you remember the music but it kind of went like this:

(*Does great impression of the music from 'Chemical Plant Zone 2'.*)

And I had these weird words that I would sing to it, I don't know why. I guess I was, like, eight at the time. The words that I would sing to the 'Chemical Plant Zone 2' song were: 'The pain that is in your face! The pain that is in your fucking, fucking f-aaace!'

I would sing it every time I was playing it! Mostly in my head, but yeah, that's a very fond memory.

On a more wholesome note, I always did love playing on Saturday mornings with my sister. We'd play *Sonic The Hedgehog 2* for ages, then maybe I'd play *Super Hang On* with my dad, and that was class.

It was just so good, man. It was a real golden time for gaming. You'd go round to a pal's house and they'd play it for ages first to show you how to do it. So many wonderful, weird memories.

A couple more questions and then I'll let you go back to sitting about in your pants eating toast or whatever it is you're doing.

Our school had its fair share of stupid challenges and dares – we would play around with the Bunsen

burners, egg folk into climbing onto the roof of our two-storey school building, pay visits to the neighbouring railway tracks and such like.

One of the stupidest games, if it could even be called that, was taking a rubber to the back of your hand and rubbing it really intensely ninety nine times, until you were bleeding. This was known as a '99-er'.

Did that ritual travel across the pond to Northern Ireland?

We had a 'chicken scratch'. Just scratching your hand ninety-nine times. And there was a guy who said that he gave himself a chicken scratch and he got to a million when blood shot out and hit the ceiling of his living room! Which I would doubt happened. I would intensely doubt that.

Pranks were massive back then. Whether it was doing a prank call or phoning an extravagant order from the local takeaway to be delivered to some unwitting sod, pulling someone's trousers down to their ankles, or something as simple as getting a pal to spell 'ICUP', there was usually some tomfoolery to be had.

What nonsense did you put each other through?

We had a few. There was all the usual; knocking around with Bunsen burners, burning pens and all that. We never had the rubber thing but like I say there was the chicken scratch which I guess was very similar.

All the old favourites; the Chinese burn. Or maybe it's the Indian burn, I'm not sure? Is that racially dubious now? It probably is. We had an ethnic burn of some kind.

A multicultural burn.

A multicultural burn. A minority burn.

One favourite was to get a large rubber and a Sharpie pen and write 'GAY' on it, back to front, and then stamp it on someone's head really hard as they're walking past.

That's right! I'd forgotten about that, man, that's brilliant!

That was a nice one.

A slightly more obscure one was my friend had this amazing, really good trick, but we did it too much to keep doing it any more. He got these bubbles, a wee tub of bubbles that you blow, and we went round the first week of school; he kept blowing them in front of first years saying 'They're edible bubbles'.

And you could just see these wee guys going 'Oh! Oh, wow!' - (*Impersonates a first year jumping around catching bubbles in his mouth*) - eating all this stuff!

People caught onto it very quickly.

One slightly horrible prank that we did have - now I never actually did this, my friend did this, I'm very quick to say - but at the time I found it funnier than I should have, and it is fairly horrible.

He'd do this thing called 'hoovering the nerds'. Which would be going to the library at lunchtime – there'd be a few guys playing games on the computer (and rightfully so, I very often was one of those guys) - but Oisin, my mate, would get this huge industrial hoover, this massive, metallic behemoth, and he'd switch it on and just hoover these guys while they were playing the computer

It was just needlessly cruel, a really horrible thing to do, but it was also satisfying watching these guys typing away, trying not to acknowledge the fact that this twelve foot hoover is in their face.

That's a terrible thing and should never be repeated by anybody...

That's the most unusual prank I think I've ever seen. He also had one called 'Lloytron', which was: in this other computer room they had this massive fan, this huge thing. It said 'Lloytron' on it. And 'Lloytron' was getting the Lloytron fan, lifting it up and going 'LLOYTRON!', blowing it right in these wee guys' faces. Not so much a prank, that's just bullying, but at least in an innovative way. I'm sure he's stopped all that now.

The best honest-to-god prank that I ever saw was on Sean, the guy who was meant to have shit himself but didn't. My mate Ben - also known as Bad Penny or Stuntman, a number of his nicknames - had devised a plan where he got two Cadbury's Creme Eggs.

It's a genius idea, executed flawlessly. He got two Cadbury's Creme Eggs. One of them he kept intact. The other one, he unwrapped the egg very carefully, making sure the paper stayed the perfect square, got the egg, put it in the freezer overnight so it was rock hard, sliced it in half really carefully with a very sharp knife, scooped out all the insides and before it had thawed again, put in a raw egg, a load of sardines, all this horrible stuff. I think there was some very poisonous stuff involved, all this noxious, terrible shit.

Before it melted again, he put the halves together very, very carefully, warmed it up with his finger, smeared the chocolate in and resealed the paper round it, really carefully, matching it so close to the original so that it really did look identical.

Of course, he now has this real egg and he now has this fake egg. A bunch of us were sitting down in the sixth form room. The only person who didn't know about this was Sean, so Ben says 'Sean, I've got a dare. I've got a bet for you. I've got two eggs here and I bet you Andy Cochrane' - who was this hulking, massive man – 'I bet you can't eat this Creme Egg faster than big Andy'.

Big Andy was in on this, completely.

Sean said: 'Of course I could. Of course I could eat it faster than him'.

They even put some arbitrary amount of money on it.

Of course, it was all going to the end result, which was Andy making a show of fumbling the paper, not being able to get his egg open, and then when he did, eating it slowly. Meanwhile, Sean's chuckling - thinking he's going to do an amazing job - tears off the wrapper, puts it into his mouth.

And I remember – it's like one of those things you see in slow motion – I remember him biting into it and all this goo and stuff just frothing out round his chin, and him just crying and crying and crying. It was just amazing, one of the most magical things I've ever seen.

I remember afterwards, the study teacher guy came in because we were making so much noise, rolling around crying. He came in to tell us off, but he was eating a banana while he was telling us off and he was eating it in a really suggestive way.

He was like: 'Do you guys think…' – and he would just suck the banana a bit for no reason – and that just fucking destroyed me! I just laughed until I was dry heaving. That's probably the best prank I've ever seen.

I've got a lot of similar things where you look back on it – you're lying in your bed at night, looking back on these things – and think that was just bullying, that was just terrible. I feel so, so bad about that.

Yes. Just terrible, terrible stuff.

And I am, of course, very curious to know what folk in your neck of the woods called it when you whipped someone's keks to the floor to expose their underpants – we called it 'skegging'…

That was called 'debagging' for us. Debagging, because your trousers are your 'bags'.

Our school, it wasn't a super-posh school, but it was maybe slightly more poncey than some. I think if you were in a rougher area of Belfast it would be 'debegging'. Bags and begs.

That's one I still hear quite a bit actually. I mentioned it the other day in work – I went into work with a backpack on and I said 'Oh sorry, I'm just going to debag myself'.

And there was a bit of giggling. But yeah, definitely still exists, debagging is what we called it.

I don't think we had as many inventive torture rituals as you did. I think ours were mostly just punching hard in the ballbag. Simple in its brutality.

I think that was what we respected the most.

XII: TEENAGE RIOT
*'You at the back! I'll not tell you again,
sit on your arse or I'll put you off the bus!'*

You're a bus driver. It's a given that you're a grumpy bastard who hates life in general, bus passengers and other road users. You believe that there is a special place in Hell for customers who pay in anything other than exact change. £20 notes send you into a wild-eyed, psychotic rampage, like Michael Douglas in *Falling Down* if he were eighteen stone and covered in crap tattoos. Your shift starts at that most unsociable of hours, 5 AM, when the inky black sky does nothing but scream that you should still be tucked up in bed.

It's winter. The roads are thick with ice and slush, extra layers of clothes do nothing to keep the freezing chill in the air at bay as you sit in your miserable little cockpit navigating the same roads for some twelve hours, day after day.

What, therefore, on God's green Earth, would possess you to take on the morning school run? Surely, as one of life's most fierce people-haters - whose patience is especially short where children are concerned - you would rather walk over a mile of hot coals than willingly escort dozens upon dozens of mad, snottery, little shits driven hyper by energy drinks and sweets chock-full of E numbers to and from school?

I have to assume that it's a lottery - that at 6 AM the country over, bus depots are full of cantankerous, overweight and balding men stood round drawing straws. I can picture the furious cursing as some poor sod takes the short straw in his grasp, the other drivers cracking their only smile of the day as they breathe a huge sigh of relief.

For our bus to St Mark's Academy, picture a prison van transporting high-risk criminals. There would be banging on the windows (sometimes as we united in song, other times for no reason other than needing to get a good bang of the windows out of your system). Fights regularly broke out, which made for the awesome spectacle of two supposed 'hard men' looking utterly ridiculous as they tried to overpower the other – or even connect a punch - whilst being rag-dolled around as the bus flew round corners and raced along at speeds of up to fifty miles per hour.

Pupils of our rival school, Kilbrenning Academy, would throw bricks at the windows. It was as if we really were inside a prison van – a prison van full of gay, black, Muslim pedophiles careening down a council estate full of angry *Daily Star* -reading UKIP voters, dodging brick after hateful brick. In the end we had to change our route, detouring to bypass Kilbrenning Academy, as the bus company eventually decided that replacing windows on a daily basis in order to shave fifteen minutes off the journey wasn't a cost-effective business model.

I assume our bus drivers underwent some sort of special forces training before taking on our run. Eventually they introduced a conductor as an extra pair of eyes and ears. It would not have been unreasonable to arm the hapless fucker with rubber bullets and tear gas.

One day, instead of a character plucked from the usual rotating cast of drivers, some poor sod – who, by his own admission, was not local - cheerfully pulled up at the stop to let us board. His first mistake was asking us schoolchildren for directions and his second, most vital mistake was taking those directions at face value. 'Aye mate, just head, err, left up here at the lights…'

It was 10.15 AM before we finally rolled up at school – with a stop for him to ask other, decent members of society for navigational help - after a detour that had taken in three other towns and the bypass to Ayr for a short spell. That was the first and last time that he did our run.

Before we even boarded the bus each day, much mischief was to be had at the bus stop.

Winter mornings would be spent having snowball fights and complaining about early starts and Baltic weather.

'My eyes are like two piss holes in the snow'.

'Ye could hang a wet duffle coat aff they nipples with two glass bottles of Irn-Bru in the pockets!'

'This is chankin'… It would freeze the baws aff a brass monkey'.

The cold weather did at least make for steamy windows and opportunities to draw body parts, or insults with arrows pointing to unsuspecting victims.

At the end of November one year, Duncan 'Cammy' Cameron arrived at the bus stop via the local shop having bought himself one of the newly-available advent calendars. He proceeded to eat all twenty four chocolates in one sitting before the bus pulled up.

In the better weather, the wait for the bus would be spent putting 'itchycoos' down the back of some sorry soul's jumper, or covering uniforms in 'sticky willies'. We would play football or graffiti the bus stop.

Best of all were mornings with wet weather. There was a dip in the plastic roof of the bus stop which would fill with rain. Paul Callaghan (the Martin Prince of the group) could always be lured into standing just outside the entrance to the bus stop, at exactly the spot the massive pool of rainwater would fall on once one of us had pushed on the roof from underneath. We caught him out with this trick dozens upon dozens of times, each time sending a huge cascade of water onto his napper.

Paul was also the butt of our jokes one morning that he came tearing round a corner and into sight, running with all his might to chase the bus that had just whizzed past him en route to our stop. We all watched as he slowed and gave a confused look from fifty yards at the fact that the bus had raced past our stop completely and that his efforts to catch it were all in vain.

He had chased the 'short bus' as it went past us on its way to the local special needs school. Kids being kids, he was never allowed to live that down.

Once we had boarded the correct bus, all that was left to sort was where we were sitting – the seats upstairs progressed from neds at the back to wild ones at the front. Downstairs it went from cool kids at the back to nerds at the front.

All Thomas and I ever cared about was racing for the seat opposite Nicola Foster, wherever that may be. She would wear short skirts and sit lengthwise with her feet on the seat, flashing her pants at the person in the seat opposite. Whether this was by default or by design, we never asked nor cared. It was a great way to help you rise in the morning.

As a matter of daily routine, our ride to school would pull into the bus roundabout at the drop-off point and we would file out of the bus for another day at St Mark's. Every single morning of my time at St Mark's can be described thusly, whether it was stepping off into rain, sunshine or snow, whether it was the height of summer or a dark winter's morning, we simply stepped off that bus and entered school without any further thought or comment.

Every morning bar one, when the bus rolled in to reveal a scene of outright carnage. Food fight.

The school janitors had gone on strike. The council

had evidently lacked the foresight to see that someone else would have to bring in the canteen's daily order of thousands of rolls from the school gates where the supplier dropped them off for the jannies to collect.

Hence, they were still sitting at the gates that morning when hundreds of pupils stepped off their buses and created a riot of epic proportions. There was a school roll of one thousand, and one thousand school rolls flying through the air as every pupil piled into the bedlam.

Throwing rolls at each other that morning is the highlight of many pupils' time at St Mark's, trumping any of the classic snowball fights we had. It turns out that thumping someone on the head with a doughy bap is immensely satisfying.

That unexpected wildness triggered something primal inside many of us. There was an unspoken agreement from there on to cause as much trouble as possible that day, a collective sense that this roll fight was only the beginning.

In a riot that would go down in St Mark's infamy as 'The Janny Strike Day', that food fight sparked chaos: bins knocked over with litter all over the school, a fire hose turned on that soaked an entire corridor, toilets flooded, a window broken and no less than six fire alarms. As was school procedure, we got marched out to line up and take part in a head count by an increasingly irate teaching staff for every single alarm, even when it became absolutely apparent to all involved that there sure as shit wasn't any fire. Much hilarity was to be had at the sight of the group of ill-fated kids in their P.E. gear who were marched out, in, out, in, out and in again during a single period.

The next day, an emergency all-school assembly was called. The head teacher lectured us for the guts of an hour. He angrily detailed everything that had gone down and the full scale of the clean-up operation. One teacher had even broken her wrist after getting trapped behind a door in a stampede.

The happy memory of deliriously running round school

corridors kicking over bins and thumping pals with breakfast rolls will forever be tainted by the horrible feeling of guilt and the memory of Mr. Anderson's disappointed face that inevitably follows it.

There was a collective feeling of shame throughout the lecture, broken only by stifled giggles as someone shouted 'Mon the jannies!' and then quickly found themselves ushered out by the scruff of their neck.

There was what felt like a controlled explosion inside my stomach. It was now or never.

'*Could I please use your bathroom?*'

I was out the door and down the corridor before the old Irish lady had even given a proper answer.

Luckily the room I raced into was in fact the bathroom. Had it instead been a linen closet, then frankly her hand towels would have had to be rewashed.

The source of my trouble had all the enthusiasm of a 100m runner doing a false start; it was turtle-necking out of my arsehole before I had even closed the door or got my trousers down.

My bum hit the loo seat and I did a stunning recreation of Harry Dunne's toilet scene from Dumb & Dumber.

I felt rocket-propelled, like I was in danger of blasting off the seat and through the roof. I opened a window to alleviate the smell, which was about as effective as poking a pinhole in the wall of a gas chamber.

What an awkward time my mum must have had just then, sitting with a stranger in her living room, making small talk to the sounds of my machine gun fire.

XIII: MY FAVOURITE GAME
'Just get a game of passy going for now...'

Place a football in the middle of any village in the world, no matter how poor or remote, and the local kids will flock to it like moths to a flame. It is the universal language and the world's favourite pastime.

Since my dad took me to my first Kilmarnock F.C. game just after my seventh birthday, I have been utterly obsessed with the greatest sport known to man. In fact, any time I get speaking to another guy and he reveals 'I don't really like football...', it's all I can do not to physically wince and ask aloud 'Well, what the fuck are we going to talk about?!'

'The fitba', as we Scots call it, has given me some of the greatest moments of my life. Reflecting on any period, there is inevitably a football memory which I recall stronger than just about any other personal milestone.

The strongest memories of my primary school days are those first few seasons of Premier League survival with Killie after our 1993 promotion. Our home ground, Rugby Park, still had terracing, and games would be spent swinging from rail to rail with friends and strangers, chasing pigeons, weaving at speed between the legs of old men, and occasionally watching the odd passage of play.

I famously missed the only goal of the game in my first visit to Rugby Park. My dad had asked me incessantly at half-time if I wanted anything from the pie stall. I told him 'No' again and again, until I spied a boy eating a Mars bar at the start of the second half. As my frustrated father bustled me along to the kiosk and out of sight of the pitch, we heard the roar that signified a Killie goal. My dad fumed, but the furore of it all bypassed me as I happily tucked into my chocolate.

Then came the emergence of my goal-scoring hero Paul Wright. Embarrassingly, I styled my hair after him, in a sort of Elvis style quiff. As a man who started going bald at the age of twenty-one, I cannot help but look back at old photos and curse what a waste I made of those few precious years in which I had hair.

My hero worship for Wright was so strong that I burst into tears of hysteria and fell speechless the first time I met him, like some young girl in the height of Beatlemania.

At a party some years later, my inner child was crushed to learn that a mate of mine knew Paul not in his days as a prolific goalscorer, but later as the driving instructor who helped him pass his test. How the mighty had fallen.

Our 1997 cup win at Ibrox, with the twenty-first minute goal from that man Wright, was the greatest day of my childhood. The only time I have been moved to tears by sport. Vivid memories of squeezing into John Finnie Street in Kilmarnock with twenty-five thousand other fans in a sea of blue and white to greet the team bus will live with me forever.

Then came a spell of six seasons, five of which saw us play in Europe against the likes of Shelbourne, Sigma Olomouc, KRR Reykjavik, OGC Nice and FC Kaiserslautern, who counted World Cup and Euro 2000 winner Yourri Djorkaeff in their ranks. He was a proud entry in an autograph book that was otherwise filled with Killie players (from the first team through to unknown lads of the youth teams), the match-day programme's cartoonist, the groundsman, and a random pub singer we had listened to in a rural Irish inn one winter.

We followed Killie home and away in those days. I remember ending up in floods of tears before one trip up to Aberdeen, upset at my mum's insistence that the only way I was travelling up to the cold east coast in mid-December was if I wore a pair of her tights underneath my trousers. Heartbroken, I eventually relented, and spent the whole match unable to concentrate on anything but the immense shame of my secret attire.

My attendance at home matches was once thrown into jeopardy by dreadful reports from one parent's evening, which resulted in my dad threatening that my season ticket would be cut to pieces if my behaviour didn't immediately and radically improve. My Maths teacher bumped into my mum some weeks later, and remarked that never in all her years of teaching had she seen such a drastic improvement in a problem pupil.

Other great memories include Scotland's wins against France in 2006 and 2007, trips following Scotland to the Republic of Ireland, Wales, England, the Netherlands, Belgium and Spain, and Kilmarnock's greatest result in my lifetime against Celtic at Hampden, in the League Cup Final of 2012.

However, my favourite football memory is undoubtedly the time I won a dream trip to the World Cup Final.

As a child, I could only dream what it would have been like to be in the USA to take in Roberto Baggio's dominant performance, in London for the crushing agony of Gazza chipping Colin Hendry and his 'dentist chair' celebration, France for the tournament-opening game in which we nearly gave world champions Brazil (and tournament star Ronaldo) a real fright, or Belgium and the Netherlands for that match between Spain and Yugoslavia.

In 2010, I finally got the chance to find out. One of the

tournament's main sponsors, Hyundai, ran a competition where the challenge was to make a video naming what you would trade in order to win a trip to the World Cup Final. I offered my collection of replica football shirts, twenty-three in all.

Included was my first ever shirt, all of my Kilmarnock and Scotland tops, as well as kits for Everton, Arsenal, both AC and Inter Milan, Paris Saint-Germain, Barcelona, Sorrento Calcio and even my local junior team, Kilbirnie Ladeside.

People could then vote for the entrant whose sacrifice they thought was most deserving of the prize. After weeks of hounding friends, family and even perfect strangers, I got the email saying I had won on Wednesday, 16th June, 2010.

Our neighbours in the flat below must have thought there was a herd of elephants doing cartwheels in our apartment as I threw my phone away in delight and started jumping around the lounge in tears, screaming at the top of my lungs. There was no one else in the house, but that didn't stop me having a celebratory rave like some reprobate from an Irvine Welsh novel monged on a tenner bag of eccies until I finally crashed on the couch, shaking, trying to slowly take it all in.

The group stage game between Spain and Switzerland was about to kick off, and it was then that I realised with a grin that what I'd prayed for in my Hyundai video could very well be about to come true: I had specifically mentioned that I wanted to see my favourite footballer of all time, Andrés Iniesta, strutting his stuff in the flesh. Spain had been my tournament team since 2000, when Scotland failed to qualify after a 1998 World Cup tournament which the nation took for granted. (If only we had known how long it would be until we qualified for another). Iniesta was to my mind the greatest player of his generation.

I watched the wee Spaniard work his magic in South

Africa on my television that afternoon while coming to terms with the fact that I'd be flying out to the country to watch a final that would, in all likeliness, feature him.

Imagine my disgust when fifty-two minutes into the match, Gelson Fernandes scored with the only Swiss attack of the game to give the underdogs victory. No sooner had I won the chance to see Iniesta and his Spanish cohorts in the flesh than the Group H leaders crashed to a shock defeat which could potentially dent their chances.

Thankfully, their campaign was soon back on track with a neat 2-1 victory over Chile in Pretoria that saw them qualify for the knockout stages. I continued to enjoy their progress through the tournament, delighted in the knowledge that in just a matter of weeks I'd be flying out to the final that they were striving to reach, all for the chance to lift the trophy for the first time in their country's history.

On the 7th July 2010, Jen and I hosted a World Cup Semi-Final party at our flat where our families cheered on Spain against Germany, and on Friday the 9th of July we flew from Glasgow to London, then London to Johannesburg, for one of the greatest weekends of our lives.

We were put up in luxury five star apartments in the posh business district of Sandton, where the locals gave odd looks to the happy Scotsman wandering around in shorts. It was South Africa's winter, but the temperature was twenty degrees Celsius and hotter than what usually passes as a British summer. I started working on a tan.

Saturday the 10th was spent at Nelson Mandela Square soaking up the pre-Final buzz. I bought a replica shirt of 'Bafana Bafana', the South African national team. I was starting a new collection of kits, since I had had to hand over three supermarket carrier bags stuffed full of cherished football strips to a Hyundai worker outside Heathrow Airport.

'Do I actually have to give these up, mate? I wasn't

sure, so I brought them with me just in case'.

'Yeah, I've been told to make sure I get them'.

'Really?'

'Yes'.

'Right. What exactly are you going to do with twenty-three football tops?'

'I've just to collect them'.

'But what happens then? I mean, I had suggested that they could be donated to a children's team in Africa'.

'No, I'm not sure. I've just to get them and take them back to the London office'.

Quite what an office full of English workers at a Japanese automobile company did with some Tesco bags full of small-sized children's Scotland shirts, one can only imagine.

On the evening of July the 10th, our first wedding anniversary, Hyundai took us out for a meal along with the other competition winners. One of the UK branch's head honchos stood up at the end of the table, toasted the twenty or so winners and informed us that dinner was on them. Best-cut steaks were ordered and hot Budweiser girls kept the beer flowing until the wee hours of the morning. A Dutch brass band randomly appeared and started entertaining diners with renditions of songs like *Carnaval de Paris*, one of my favourite songs of all time. The incredible day we enjoyed before the matchday would itself have been a great top prize in any other competition.

On the Sunday morning, we rubbed shoulders in Johannesburg with an assortment of well-known faces whose passing-by just drove home how extraordinary it was for a couple of ordinary punters from Ayrshire to be at such an event: Andy Townsend, Edwin Van Der Saar, Gareth Southgate, Mark Lawrenson, Vincent Del Bosque, Brian Bowey, Ray Parlour, Frank Skinner, David Baddiel, Jim Rosenthal and Raymond Van Barneveld to name but a few.

The one time I was genuinely star-struck came when I

caught sight of Kenny Dalglish, Scotland legend. I couldn't resist pestering him for a photograph. He is every bit as grumpy as people would have you believe, but he nutmegged Ray Clemence at Hampden, so I can forgive the man a lack of personality.

On the coach to the game later that day, a Hyundai rep walked the length of the bus handing lucky winners their precious golden briefs. It was then that we learned of one final surprise: we were to enjoy luxury pre and post -match hospitality. For several hours before the game, we helped ourselves to as much free food and alcohol as possible in the sponsor's exclusive hospitality lounge. Not bad for a man whose pre-match meal is usually nothing more than a Killie Pie and a couple of cheap pints of cider in Rugby Park's Sports Bar.

We entered the stadium a couple of hours before kick-off time in order to watch the opening ceremony, a stunning display of fireworks, dancing and pop star Shakira's spectacular arse shaking about in all its glory.

Incredibly, we also witnessed what would transpire to be Nelson Mandela's last ever public appearance, as they wheeled the then ninety-two year old out on the back of a golf buggy for a quick spin around the turf. It was monumental enough that I paused on my way to the queue for beers to witness it. Unlike Shakira, Madiba didn't shake his booty or indeed bust any sort of move, which was a little disappointing to be honest.

Finally we took our seats, with Category 1 tickets which saw us situated just seven rows from the front and almost bang in line with the half-way line, and witnessed a piece of football history. Spain v Netherlands, the World Cup Final 2010.

When 'El Ilusionista', Andrés Iniesta, popped up with a half-volley in the 27th minute of extra time, my journey had come full circle. There wasn't a Spaniard in the stadium who went as nuts as I did.

It was something I had dreamed of doing, or at the

very least witnessing, since I was a child. Here I was, at a World Cup Final, watching a hero of mine score the all-important goal; a goal which would go down in the record books. It was an unbelievable experience.

As though to confirm just how obsessed with football I am, the next match I went to after the World Cup Final was a slightly less glamorous tie later that month; a pre-season junior football friendly between Irvine Vics and Kilbirnie Ladeside attended by around twenty people and the proverbial man and his dog.

One of the things I love most about Scottish football is the banter to be had at such games. What our fixtures lack in skill or moments of spellbinding footballing ability, they more than make up for with witty shouts full of Scottish humour from the crowd.

Take, for example, a Ladeside game I attended some years ago where the opposition goalkeeper kept falling on his arse during his goal kicks, due to slippery conditions. After yet another tumble, the roar from a punter behind me went: 'Haw you, ya useless bastard, can you no stay on yer feet? They'd be better off with Douglas Bader in nets, ya goofy prick'.

From then on in, the poor lad had to play the rest of the game subject to a torrent of abuse from the stands comparing him to the World War II pilot who famously lost his legs. He went on to ship another three goals, falling on his arse repeatedly - perhaps not surprisingly - in the process.

Or what about the match I was at in the 1990s between Kilmarnock and Rangers where a full stadium joined in with a chorus aimed at one foolish Gers fan?

The stadium was quiet at half-time, but for the low muttering of fans discussing the game and tucking in to their well-renowned Killie Pies, which regularly win football grub accolades. It was at this point that a Rangers fan stood up in the away end and, clear as day, shouted across at the home support: 'Killie, yer pies are SHITE!'

Quick as a flash, a fan near me pounced with the brilliant reply of 'Aye, and you look like you ate them all, ya fat cunt!'

Cue some twelve thousand fans from both sides joining in with a gleeful rendition of *Who Ate All The Pies?* as the overweight Rangers supporter in question meekly took his seat again.

Unfortunately, while I love watching the great game, it quickly became apparent to me as a child that no amount of effort, practice or training was going to change my abundant lack of talent. As my dad bluntly put it, 'Ye can only pish with the cock you've got, son'.

Or as another favourite father of mine would say, 'You tried your best and you failed miserably. The lesson is, never try'.

What's most baffling of all about this is that I had a football education that should have stood me in good stead.

Around the world, children learn football in all manner of different ways. In Brazil they play barefoot. French kids play games on the beach in nothing but shorts. Spanish kids learn intricate passing triangles and close control in the game futsal, played with a smaller ball on tighter pitches.

In their search for the perfect coaching model, football associations around the world try to analyse what impact these massively different styles have on players.

I defy any football expert to explain how I and the rest of the kids who played football in St. Margaret's Avenue did not go on to be superstars. Our touch, close control, ability to navigate challenges; all perfectly honed, as we plied our craft at the 'Two Trees'.

The Two Trees was an imaginatively-titled, small patch of grass which boasted, not surprisingly, two trees. It was roughly fifteen foot by fifteen foot. In a cinch, the grass could be used as an okay pitch for games of two-a-side, all too common in those days.

What more often happened is that the imaginary markings of the pitch were stretched out to include the opposite, similar-sized patch of grass.

The only problem was that this additional patch of grass lay on the other side of a road. Between the two patches of grass was a junction, which sat at the top of a steep hill. To the side of each patch was the St. Margaret's Avenue road, running parallel, and down the middle ran the vertical line of the T junction, Peden Avenue.

Simply scoring a goal required precision dribbling, close control, strength, vision, and the ability to avoid not only tackles but an assortment of disruptive and dangerous vehicles.

The average goal went something like this:

The goalkeeper played the ball out to you. After beating a player, you almost lost control of the ball at the other side of him, faced with the small concrete lip that framed the grass. Quickly, you would roll it over that obstacle and onto the pavement, always wary of oncoming opposition; a tackle whilst dealing with the transition from grass to pavement was certain to lose you possession.

Now, you were tasked with bumping down from the pavement, off the kerb and down on to the road - which was at the top of a very steep hill. If you were lucky enough to find the junction free of cars - you seldom checked before entering, instead relying on the game-pausing shout of 'Car!' from another player - you could continue across the road, doubtless facing at least one challenge from a defending player.

This was the most important tackle of all to ride. Any contact and the ball would roll for a hundred yards or more down the slope of Peden Avenue, leading to the frequent argument of whose responsibility it was to chase down after it.

At the other side of the road, the thankless feat was

repeated - over the pavement kerb, across the lip around the grass, and back onto terra firma. From the left, you could switch the play to your teammate, but you would have to complete your pass while avoiding the first of the two trees.

Having successfully navigated that, your pass would reach the other flank and your mate - himself dealing with an obstructive tree. His touch would have to be up to scratch to receive the ball, avoid the tree and skirt round any oncoming players. Having skinned any defenders and both trees, a one-two would see you in on goal, where you still had to keep your nerve in order to score. If you did manage to beat the keeper after such a taxing route to goal, celebrations were wild. Understandably, games were low scoring and those rare scoring opportunities taken were hailed with fervour, celebrated with a Ravanelli-style shirt-over-the-head moment.

Goalposts at the Two Trees were marked out thus; jumpers for goalposts, a large, wooden fence in place of a net, with the top of the fence serving as a crossbar. Any shot blasted above the highest part of the fence was deemed 'over'.

Unfortunately there was no point, save for ground-level where our clothes lay, at which the exact location of the posts were clear. Raging feuds over what was 'in' were commonplace. Debates would also break out over if, had the post been a real, tangible stanchion, would the ball actually have went 'in off the post'?

In games without a solid wall or fence to play against, the exact height of the crossbar would vary on a case by case basis, with the height of the goalkeeper and whether he could have conceivably reached the shot the only considerations. The imaginary crossbar could literally move up and down and up again several times during a match if we were taking turns at 'one and out'.

Games at the Two Trees were regularly interrupted by Mrs. Humphrey, whose house was on the other side of the fence we used as a goal. A fence, I might add, which proclaimed 'No Ball Games' in big bold letters.

Her name was absolute muck with us young lads. Any time she appeared to complain about the noise of a ball banging incessantly against her fence, we would give her torrents of cheeky abuse and ignore her pleas for us to play elsewhere. One time we even pelted the side of her house with handfuls of muck as payback for her stealing our ball.

In hindsight, she was just a poor old woman who wanted to sit peacefully in her front room without cries of 'Ball squared across! He jumps for the volley... DI CANIOOOOO!' and the constant sound of a size five Mitre rattling against our makeshift goal.

She lived the sad life of a widowed pensioner, watching television and filling in crosswords, and only wanted some peace and quiet in which to while away her final, lonely years without the local boys turning her fence and neighbouring grass into a matchday Hampden.

Still... Fuck her.

The chaos of sorting out teams for these games was everyone's least favourite part of any kickabout. Without a coach or teacher to mix players in a balanced and impartial manner, we kids would regularly come to blows over what the teams were and how to sort them, with cries of 'No fair! No fair!' ringing out.

With the game over and kids making their way home, players from the losing team would invariably get together and mutter 'Aye, but the teams weren't fair', with all the decorum of Arsene Wenger moaning about Financial Fair Play.

There were two common methods for picking sides.

Two captains would be nominated (even selecting these roles caused arguments, with the usual resolution being that it should be owner of the ball and the best player to pick) and then took turns to choose players. Being chosen last hurt like a knife to the gut and to this day I can still recognise that same masked torment on the face of 'last pick' children. Studies have (probably) shown that kids chosen last at football are more likely to become mass murderers in later life.

Picking numbers was the best way to make randomised teams. 'You turn your back and I'll dae numbers' was the cry. Once every player had been assigned a number, the person who had turned their back looked round, called out two sets of numbers and pointed to the half of the pitch which these players should take. Odds and evens was the usual choice of the unimaginative.

En route to a kickabout, my best mate Thomas and I would often pre-determine how these supposedly random numbers were going to go, to ensure we ended up in the same team. 'You offer to do the numbers and I'll turn my back. You be 1 and I'll be 2...'

In fact, as adults we sometimes still pull off this move with success at five-a-side games, with the other players either unsuspecting or simply not caring about how the teams are made for an hour-long friendly kickabout.

With a hodge-podge mix of football shirts on show, there was only one way to make the two teams distinctly different: shirts vs. skins. Thus, one wee group of boys would play with their best replica gear on, while the other ran about half-naked, making for one hell of a sight for any passing neighbours.

Almost as soon as teams were decided, shouts of 'Turn around, touch the ground, I'm not in' would break out. Whoever was last to announce this, whilst literally spinning and putting a hand to their toes, had effectively just nominated themselves for a stint in nets.

In games with fewer players, this issue could be overcome either by permitting 'Goalies allowed out' – the rule that keepers could temporarily step outfield for solo runs and scoring goals – or 'First man back', a chaotic system that allowed for any outfield player to keep goal based only on who gets there first whilst defending.

'Hand ball!'

'Naw, remember we've got any man-er!'

Goalkeepers would be protected by a couple of important rules: no poaching and no blasties.

The first was a rudimentary offside rule which meant players weren't allowed to simply hang around in the opposition's six yard box. This was usually the domain of fat lads, who would stand there happily munching a bag of crisps while a game broke out around them, becoming animated only when the ball came within three yards of their shooting foot.

No blasties, meanwhile, meant goals could be chopped off if you had dared to hit the ball so hard that the opposition keeper had been inclined to dive away from it rather than towards.

The next cause for argument – because, like professional football, there was more of an emphasis on petulant squabbling than there was on actually kicking a football around – was who you were going to 'be'. Each player would effectively pretend to be a famous professional for the course of the game, channelling anyone from Ronaldo (now 'Fat Ronaldo' to avoid confusion with Cristiano) or Maldini to Gazza or Eoin Jess.

Your chosen player would be a telling reflection of how you saw your own playing style. Those who fancied themselves as poachers would pick well-known goalscoring heroes like Alan Shearer, while anyone who thought they were good enough to 'pull the strings' in a match might opt for someone like Juan Sebastian Veron or Paul Scholes. Part of the fun then lay in aping their scoring celebration. On pitches around the UK, wee boys in the nineties were banging in goals then running around with one arm held aloft, paying homage to Shearer.

Clearly, and this was the most important thing, there could only be two Ronaldos. That is to say, there could be the actual Ronaldo and one player in your game copying his style. It almost went without saying that once someone had decreed that they were impersonating their chosen professional, a second player could not then pick the same person. What sort of anarchy would break out if two young boys on a council park in the west of Scotland both pretended to be Ally McCoist in the same game? Impossible.

What's more, players could also juggle their new-found role as player imitator with that of running commentator. 'Caniggia, megs one, feints out wide, cuts inside onto his favoured foot, looks up, shoots, OHHHHHHHHHH, it's a goal! Spectacular! The crowd goes wild!'

There were many other unwritten rules which governed our games. I couldn't believe, for instance, when Nathan Dyer and Jonathan de Guzman nearly came to blows over who was to take a penalty in the English League Cup Final in February 2013. Dyer wanted his hat-trick, de Guzman was the nominated penalty taker, and in the middle of Wembley in front of 82,000 fans in a match that they were winning 3-0 against Bradford, the Swansea players had a roaring argument. Whatever happened to 'makers takers'? Our simple rule that whoever won the penalty, hit the penalty, ensured no such arguments broke out amongst us kids. It's absolutely baffling that professional footballers couldn't abide by that same playground law.

Another important thing that we all agreed on was that whoever got the last touch had to go fetch the ball whenever it soared out of play.

'You touched it last, mate.'

Boys would regularly be seen disappearing into thickets of bushes, nearby woods or neighbours' gardens in order to retrieve a stray ball. Lads the country over remember the day that their mate disappeared into the bushes only to reappear holding aloft a discarded porno mag. Teams came together to huddle round for what was many boys' first look at a pair of tits and the game - even the lost ball - was roundly forgotten about.

The first time I realised how widespread this

phenomenon is was when stand-up comic Kevin Bridges riffed on the matter in his set. I remembered our own experience all too well and was doubled over to hear a stranger reciting what I thought of as my story. I've since discussed the matter with loads of pals and to a man, they each have their own version of this wonderful memory.

'Match abandoned!'

Any retrievals of lost balls from stranger's gardens (hopefully) involved far less nudity and usually required two players; the one whose last touch had nominated them for fetching duties, and a loyal friend. The latter would have the job of simply knocking the door, while the former had the unenviable task of 'doing the talking', asking some grumpy old bastard for their ball back. 'I'll knock, you talk'. Many an elderly gardener built a store of knifed, burst footballs in his shed and would knock back your pleading requests with an angry rant. Pricks, the lot of them.

Goalkeepers seldom took a stint of retrieving the ball, preferring instead to cry 'Play on'. Players who would normally have had rip-roaring spats over fetching the ball would then race to get it, trying to dribble it back onto the field of play for another shot at goal.

With no ref, penalties were normally only given if someone had been taken away in an ambulance with a snapped leg. It also meant that there was no one to call time, so games would typically end only when it was too dark to see, a fight had broken out or the owner of the ball had taken umbrage to something and gone home.

As well as the obvious rule that overrode all others – 'It's ma baw!' – there was also a stipulation that said no new ball could be used on concrete for the first month after purchasing.

'Use that one, it's better'.

'Naw, it's just new. I don't want the bits coming off'.

'Alright, fair enough', was usually how it went. Everyone could well imagine the wrath their own mum would rain down had they come home with their brand new World Cup ball missing a panel of leather, so that was that.

Any player joining in with an older gang of kids – no matter if the age gap was only a year or so - would be handled with kid gloves, being allowed to do everything from taking kick-ins instead of throw-ins, to hitting penalties from half the distance. Anyone fouling the young one would be remanded as a 'saddo' and there would be great debate as to whether an imaginary red card should be brandished.

The worst dilemma that we ever faced was when an older guy came past and asked for - or demanded - a kick of the ball. A snap assessment of his 'hardness' was made and then the only question was whether to kick it to him, or 'bolt'.

Games could be wrapped up with a simple shout of 'Next goal the winner', usually invoked by the side behind by five.

Conversely, school playground games could be extended by a cry of 'Play on after the bell!' A line of wee boys with mucky uniforms, looking like something out of a Persil advert, would then be marched back into their respective classrooms by an angry head teacher refusing to believe the protestations of 'We never heard it, Sir, honest!'

For the sake of the five minutes we had spent trying to finish our epic game, the teacher would then waste a further twenty minutes bemoaning the waste of class time, the hypocritical old wench.

When there were too few players for teams - or a game had fallen apart because the cry was 'These teams are no fair!'- a game of 'Cuppy' would break out instead. Whether 'singles' or 'doubles', Cuppy was a game where players would all shoot into one goal.

'Two and through'.

You, or you and your doubles partner, would have to net two goals past the keeper in order to go through to the next round: the round would continue until all but one player had done this, the loser would be eliminated, and a new round would start. The final usually involved 'Three goals the winner!' and the knocked-out players from previous rounds would gather round the pitch cheering and jeering to create a bit of atmosphere.

'Headers and Volleys' was another game that involved players shooting into the same goal. A wide man would provide crosses while the other players tried to beat the keeper with either a header or a volley. If the goalie saved any striker's effort, they would throw the ball to another player – if that person's header or volley went in, the original striker then had to keep nets.

How all of this – the improvised pitches, the skill-honing games, the twenty-a-side neighbourhood matches and the constant desire to be like our footballing idols – could somehow fail to make superstar players of us all is a mystery to me.

Even just the fact that a ball was pretty much glued to our feet throughout the whole of the 1990s should surely have counted for something.

But no, in spite of all of this, I have very limited ability when it comes to actually playing football. I run out onto the pitch for ninety minutes of total commitment, with all the passion in the world, to work hard and chase down every ball; but the skill simply isn't there. Those characteristics were enough to win Kenny Miller sixty-nine caps, but I am sadly still waiting on a call-up to the national side.

However, that's not to say my football career has been without its glory.

Growing up, every football fan on the planet daydreams of captaining their side at the club's home ground, their goalscoring heroics celebrated by a vocal partisan crowd at fever pitch. Not many ever get the chance to.

I did.

On a day that will live long in the memory, I had the incredible honour of pulling on the armband and stepping out at Rugby Park, home of Kilmarnock Football Club.

A noisy home support roared me on as, mid-match, I expertly took a touch to control the ball on that hallowed turf, beat a couple of players, and looked up for a sight at goal. I felt the expectant eyes of the crowd waiting to see what I would do next.

Like in the best of sports movies, these vital, match-changing moments truly do happen in slow motion. I had all the time in the world to weigh up the options as the action slowed down to a snail's pace: behind me, for an easy pass, were defenders in complete safety; to my left and right, wingers ready to take on the full backs; ahead of me our striker, crying out for the ball.

The last option was the lowest percentage possibility, a completely speculative shot from distance - I was just behind the halfway line at the time. To shoot was madness.

Instinct told me that the goalkeeper wasn't ready. No defence in the world would have been prepared for what I did next. I knew I just had to connect sweetly: get it on target and the surprise of it all might just see the ball sneak in.

I struck it with all my might.

The ball soared through the air, hanging in a way that seemed to defy the laws of physics. The coaching staff, my team, the opposition, the crowd and I; we all looked on, helpless, just waiting expectantly to see where the ball would go.

It continued to move through the air, towards goal. As we all watched, only the goalkeeper had the power to do anything now.

But the keeper saw it late. As it sailed over their head, the crossbar was the last thing standing between me and glory.

The ball struck the bar. Rugby Park held its collective

breath.

It flew down, and in. Goal!

I had scored from behind the halfway line at my place of worship, the home stadium of my beloved football team. I had achieved the dream of boys across the world.

The fans went wild, my teammates wilder. I was mobbed in an instant, suddenly losing sight of the angry goalkeeper picking the ball out of the opposition net, lost underneath a chaotic pile of the players I captained.

If all of this sounds too good to be true, I can promise that it really did happen.

There are details that perhaps take some of the shine off the whole thing: I was ten at the time, playing for the Dalry team in a cross-county kids' tournament, and was chosen as captain only because I happened to be the one Killie fan in the team, the one player for whom the venue, Rugby Park, would have significance; the crowd of around fifty or so onlookers inside the 18,000-seater stadium were made up of coaches and parents of the kids involved; we were playing on a smaller, makeshift pitch going across the full pitch, with goalposts set up on either touchline; our opposition was an all-girls team who were a year younger, and whose goalkeeper was not even half the height of the goals; my goal from behind the halfway line was one of more than a dozen in a match we eventually won 13-0.

However - insignificant minutiae aside - no one can take away from me the fact that I, as captain, scored from behind the halfway line at the home of my beloved Kilmarnock, with the home crowd's cheers ringing in my ears. In fact, if I listened hard enough, I could even make out the overly-enthusiastic yells of my mum.

XIV: THIS IS HARDCORE
'Foot was on the rope! Ma shoulder's up!'

At the end of sunny days, school clothes would smell of a heady mix of grass, sweat and other children's blood. Enjoying massive popularity in those days, wrestling was the cause of this uniform vandalism, and the definition of a 'water cooler' topic for us boys; if you hadn't seen that weekend's *Raw* and *Smackdown*, couldn't discuss the latest main event and weren't willing to throw down a few imitation moves of your own in the playground battles that broke out, you were about as popular as Vince McMahon.

We were old enough to know that it was all 'as choreographed as any ballet', as Lisa Simpson once put it, but weren't yet cynical enough to care.

Due to taking place in America with its different time zone, monthly pay-per-views were broadcast in the wee hours of Sunday night, meaning every boy had to struggle with the timer on his VCR to record the whole thing to video. Monday morning rises many hours before school started were not uncommon, in order to watch the latest three-hour long event.

Those who couldn't face such an early rise – myself included – had to fast-forward to the end over breakfast (something I hated doing) or simply avoid news of how the headline fight had turned out. Most kids were willing to bite their tongue for those poor souls who couldn't face the pre-6am start, but there was always one sniveling little shit who would smugly describe in great detail how The Rock had pinned Triple H to the sound of your pleading cries. That afternoon was spent half-heartedly watching *Survivor Series*, cursing the prick who had ruined it and pledging to pull an 'all-nighter' for the next one.

That WWF broadcast these programs with its 'Don't try this at home' warning meant very little to us, a group of half-wit idiots who would copy the most fatal of stunts if it made us cool. Besides, did they mention anything about trying it in school playgrounds? Wrestling bouts resulted daily in cuts, bumps and even breaks but McMahon and his suits needn't worry: how could anyone hold some faraway corporation liable when we were busy keeping hush-hush and denying word of our outlawed bouts to teachers and other school staff? Injuries had to be taken on the chin or simply lied about, for anything else would be grassing, and admitting knowledge to the 'heidy' of some shady inner-school wrestling organisation operating on school grounds.

'The first rule of Fight Club is: You do not talk about Fight Club. The second rule of Fight Club is: You do not talk about Fight Club'.

Of course, nothing was actually well-organised where these fights were concerned. There was no prior thought, no bill of events, not even a physical belt for which to compete; just an imaginary title to be held aloft at the end of a good three-count.

Quite simply, the sun peeking out from the clouds, or the grass of our school fields being cut, was sign enough that it was time for another round of fighting. Wordlessly, boys would converge on the playing fields, kids would take on characters, storylines would be dreamt up in an instant, and total fucking chaos would break out.

Our matches could best be described as adopting the 'battle royal' format. Where the pros were eliminated in battle royal by being sent outwith the ropes around the ring – if their feet touched the floor surrounding the ring, they were out - we were eliminated in the usual manner by three-count pin or submission (tapping out to a chokehold or similar submission move). Picture the thirty-wrestler bedlam of a *Royal Rumble* event and our lunchtime football field comes clearer into view. Discarded jumpers lay dotted amidst the bodies, ties were used in strangleholds, school bags became weapons.

Unofficial rules included a '24/7' allowance similar to that of the WWF's Hardcore Championship. That is, our wrestling title could be challenged at any time, any place within school grounds. Word of title wins would spread secretly around the circuit of known grapplers, keeping everyone in the loop on the identity of the current holder. News of a fresh champion always created a buzz and sparked ideas of how you could catch the new title holder when he least expected it.

Accordingly, some of the best bouts broke out in ludicrous places: the assembly hall, school corridors, even the boys' toilet. Everywhere was fair game. Teachers would often have to charge en masse to the library, the lunch hall, even the oratory (a designated prayer space in our Catholic school) on one mad occasion, to contain and break up unannounced scraps that had bust out as someone caught the current champ unawares in a challenge of their title.

Champions would often have to call on 'hauners' – a small circle of friends who could be relied upon not to challenge but instead to jump into fights on his side – just to help keep the onslaught of relentless attackers manageable. Once one wrestler had started a challenge, 'battle royal' mentality kicked in and everyone and anyone could join in; mostly piling in on the champion, but with separate non-title fights breaking out as delirium arose.

These unplanned wrestling matches would often start with one man's well-planned challenge in a quiet corridor developing into an all-out brawl with contestants piling in unannounced as word spread.

As with so many fantastic school memories, this was a ritual seemingly shared amongst the schools of so many of my now-friends across Scotland. My mate Cattigan recalls identical madness; our exact format, those same unofficial rules and very similar memories, set in an unrelated school many miles away.

His own personal highlight was the time someone DDT-ed him down some stairs.

Most amazing of all his wrestling recollections is undoubtedly the time his mate Aaron got suspended from school.

Like so many other breaks, this particular playtime had descended into pandemonium with Rock Bottoms, Pedigrees and Choke Slams being dealt out next to the tuck shop. In the anarchy, tuck sweets were being tossed around by participants and eager onlookers alike. Dozens of wee guys were steaming in to some poor bugger desperately defending his title. More and more pupils charged down the corridor at word of this to enjoy the ensuing fracas, shouts of legendary commentator JR Ross' trademark 'It's a slobberknocker!' cry ringing out round the halls.

Cattigan's mate Aaron was in the mix. While at his feet lay two boys in the throes of a Crippler Crossface, one trying with all his might not to tap out, to his side another held a poor victim by the arms for some friend to fire in with knee blows to the stomach. An attacker came at Aaron from the front and it was all he could do to battle away the arms as they arranged themselves around him into that familiar pose which meant an incoming Rock Bottom.

That challenge successfully avoided, he was suddenly grabbed from behind in the melee. On instinct, he half-turned to get his bearings, gripped the head of the attacker in his peripheral vision in a hold, and threw the pair downwards, excitedly hitting out with that immortal word we all loved so well: 'Stunner!'

Executed perfectly, the 'Stone Cold Stunner' made famous by fan-favourite Steve Austin would get the opponent's face locked into position above the wrestler's shoulder as they dropped to a seated position on the floor, brutally slamming the opponent's jaw into the shoulder at the point of impact.

Rising on a high, pumped and ready for his next scrap, Aaron jumped to his feet and tried to pick out the next target in the heaving throng of uniformed bodies.

As he did so, however, an alien silence began to spread slowly through the usually-cacophonous crowd of battered bodies. Moves were abandoned, embraces dropped, submission holds simply broken up without a winner.

Amidst it all, the current champion stood undefeated, mouth agape.

Aaron was at the heart of this scene, least informed of all. Trying to process the situation and understand what unseen signal had stopped the brawl, he spun worriedly, and at 180 degrees the absolute horror that struck him to his core can only be part-imagined.

There on the floor in front of him, writhing around in the agonising aftermath of his Stone Cold Stunner, lay Mr. McEneaney, History teacher – a poor man who had obviously been trying to seize participating kids in order to contain the situation.

What a magnificent letter home that must have been.

Shawn Michaels vs. Razor Ramon in *Wrestlemania X*'s Ladder Match. Stone Cold Steve Austin vs. The Rock for the WWE Championship in a No DQ match at *Wrestlemania XVII*. *Royal Rumble 2001*.

None of these classic 'slobberknockers' are remembered as fondly in Johnstone High School as the time Aaron got wrestling banned and himself suspended with a monumental Stunner on a teacher. Horrific at the time, but surely worth the massive punishment and criminal reputation to be forever known as the guy who nearly got a three-count on Mr. McEneaney.

XV: GUILTY CONSCIENCE
'It's not big and it's not clever'.

We recently bought our first house. While I have begrudgingly come to accept that I am now more than a decade on from my childhood – with the wife, car, job, house and new baby to reaffirm as much – there is still an inner child cursing me for taking out a fixed-rate mortgage, instead of making a game out of running in front of cars, or railing at the thought of taking out a life insurance policy rather than hiding in bushes and throwing berries at random passers-by.

In time, we came to love the house, but the first few months were miserably spent decorating (including, thankfully, wallpapering over a diarrhea-yellow wall), clearing out loose dog food that we found lying around in cupboards, and forking out several grand in boiler and heating repairs.

All of this meaning my inner child had further cause to complain. In protest, I spent money I had been given for my birthday and Christmas – with a little more pinched from our savings on top – to set up a home cinema in the study.

If mornings were to be spent making phone calls in

order to switch energy providers and doing other such monotonous tasks, evenings would at least involve a seventy inch screen, the misadventures of a certain yellow family, and a subwoofer that would shake the entire room. Adult Life 1, Inner Child 1.

It was on one of the first nights we spent in our new home that I came to realise just how awful 102C and I had been to Mrs. McMillan, our Geography teacher. As I lay in bed staring at the ceiling (and deciding then that it needed a fresh coat of paint), unable to sleep for unseen whistlers, I felt nothing but empathy for the woman we drove to quitting St. Mark's.

Scrambling around somewhere above my head were a family of birds. From the loft came intermittent noises – wings fluttering, beaks scratching, tiny feet tapping and most annoyingly of all, bloody sing-song whistling – that confirmed there was a nest in there.

Always out of sight but never out of mind. Perfectly audible, whilst totally unseen. Whistle, whistle, whistle: just as it had been for Mrs. McMillan on that fateful day that we made her swear at us.

Whenever I watch quiz shows, I curse that my geography lets me down so badly. Deep down I know I only have myself to blame.

Funnily enough, I don't remember what Mrs. McMillan was teaching us that day. Her lesson, as she preached to us from the whiteboard, got lost somewhere in a cacophony of high-pitched noise.

It started off, as these things so often did, with Daryl Allison. The lesson involved short periods of teacher talking directly to us, invariably followed by the need to turn back to the whiteboard and write something up.

Daryl and a few of the other class goons saw the opportunity to whistle every time McMillan turned her back to us to face the whiteboard. A few whistles, the odd giggle around the room and a teacher who eventually acknowledged it with a cheerful 'Come on, now'.

Many years later, I was camping at a festival down in England when we got talking to some random Scottish folk around the campfire. After several ciders, we moved onto reminiscing about school stories, as you do.

Upon realising that one girl went to Kilbrenning Academy, the other secondary school in town, I enthusiastically piped up 'Oh, you'll know Mrs. McMillan then!' and told this very story.

Sensing that Mrs. McMillan was going to continue to turn round to the whiteboard, a few more brave souls took part.

The worst behaved boy had started it. His comrades soon followed suit. As the game grew, Chris Hamilton, Gerry Daniels and I – decent kids but all easily led – started whistling too. Last to whistle were the good girls who only took part out of peer pressure. A few prim and proper girls sat steadfast, refusing to be drawn in to the growing whistle mob.

My now sister-in-law Katrina was one of the few who stayed silent. She went on to win various awards in university, including one for best degree results nationwide, while I only recently realised that the Clyde Tunnel in Glasgow runs beneath the River Clyde ('There's water above us right now? Wow!'). She probably made the right choice, but whatever.

It went from a couple of quick peeps every few minutes to full-blown mayhem, with twenty kids at a time holding their whistles until she spun back to face the class. Her cheeks flushed and she started to become genuinely annoyed.

'Will you all stop whistling, please?!'

Five minutes later, having been battered into submission with waves of whistling, she started repeating one phrase, a slight on our maturity. I remember vividly how she said over and over: 'Grow up!'

Like a classroom full of Peter Pan pricks, we didn't. The only thing that grew was the noise level. The classroom started to sound like a sheepdog convention. Eventually the whole episode became a farce and it was impossible for the lesson to continue. Game over. Match abandoned.

Truly pissed off now, she sat at her desk, made us take out our books and told us to turn to a certain page. If we were going to behave like children she would treat us like children, apparently. She gave us some menial task like copying a whole page into our jotters and sat watching the class intently.

Looking back, the most surprising thing of all is that we continued. I can say honestly that there would not have been one pupil in that class who disliked Mrs. McMillan. She was a lovely teacher, a genuinely nice person. The chink in her armour was that she was too soft, too easily wound up, and that was something 102C found irresistible…

When I used to goad my sister for fun, my dad would tell her: 'He's winding you up. Don't give him a reaction and he'll soon get bored'.

Mrs. McMillan would have done well to realise that herself.

There was a temporary respite of about five minutes as we readjusted to this new situation. McMillan sat at her desk, eyeballing us intently. To whistle, we now had to glance furtively from our book to check if she was watching. A quick peep, enough that she couldn't catch you with a flick of her eyes.

One whistle would take her eyes glancing to the protagonist, left. That was an opportunity for five boys sat on the right of the class – five quick whistles and now she was looking for them, hopeless. Clearly it had come from that side of the room – but with lightning reflexes, they had again buried their heads in the textbooks, and no culprit presented himself.

She looked all round, increasingly mad, always one step behind the whistlers. Each whistle would create cover for another.

It came to a head. One last whistle pushed her over the edge. She stood up and gave us all the fright of our lives as she suddenly shouted: 'Bastards! Bastards! Shut up!'

She ran into a cupboard and slammed the door behind her to a chorus of hysterical laughter.

We had made a teacher swear! Magic!

Like the animals we were, we all started battering the desks in a drum roll and, of course, whistling.

This continued for a few minutes. The noise subsided instantly as the depute heads, Mr. McPhee and Mr. Moffat, appeared. Evidently, Mrs. McMillan had used a phone in the store cupboard to call for 'hauners'. Grassbag.

Mr. McPhee watched as Mr. Moffat went into the cupboard to check on poor Mrs. McMillan. Believe it or not, we took that as a cue for one last round of whistling. We really were a shower of bastards.

Needless to say, the depute heads went absolutely 'tonto'. There was silence, shame, a few red faces. I'm not going to lie, there were a few suppressed giggles too, but these were roundly jumped upon by Moffat and McPhee, and after a good, long lecture which made us see how cruel it had been, none of us had anything to say but 'Sorry'.

All the talk in the playground for the next couple of days was how 102C had made a teacher swear!

Sitting in a field at that English festival some time later, the reason I assumed that girl would know Mrs. McMillan is because soon after the whistling incident, she moved to Kilbrenning Academy – where, as I had learned earlier, this girl had been a pupil. 102C would forever carry the reputation that we had driven away a teacher and made her change schools, whether that was the real reason or not.

After recounting my story, I proudly sat back in my camping chair and asked if the girl knew McMillan, the teacher we had driven to madness with our whistling.

'Yes', the girl said, her expression giving nothing away. 'She's my mum'.

That was the moment I realised, as my face turned redder than the evening sunset and my inane grin slowly melted into a shameful frown, what a horrible, horrible shit I am. That was the moment that 'The time we whistled until McMillan swore at us, ran into a cupboard and moved schools' was removed from my mental list of happy childhood memories and filed instead under regrets that will haunt me for the rest of my life.

I am a bad person. The birds in the loft keeping me up at night with their whistling? Karma.

The Irish lady's bathroom had been obliterated. She would have to hang an 'Out Of Order' sign on the door and just forget this room ever existed.

For that matter, I ought to hang a 'Bang Out Of Order' sign on my arse. What had just happened down there was an absolute disgrace.

I sat resting, completely drained, ashamed of the ungodly smell but not yet able to move. The poor woman had thought I was just spending a penny, when in fact I had deposited my entire life savings.

That much was certainly common knowledge. The five required flushes had seen to that. Her and my mum were in no doubt as to what had gone down in here, although there was simply no way they could imagine the full extent of the atrocity.

Thankfully I had been able to find a new roll of toilet paper when required. No need to decimate her bath mat or shower curtain into the bargain.

I gingerly left the toilet seat and prepared to do the walk of shame.

XVI: ORIGINAL PRANKSTER
'It's all fun and games until someone gets hurt'.

The first thing that hits you after someone pulls your trousers down to your ankles in public is the fact that the world at large can see your underpants. This realisation often takes a moment; any good schoolboy prank should be so shocking, performed so unexpectedly, that its victim is left for a time trying gormlessly to process 'What's going on?' whilst mates and strangers alike point and laugh.

As the victim hoists their trousers back up in as quick a time as possible, fumbling in their rush, the hilarity sweeping around them acts as a painful reminder that no boy with aspirations to be popular reacts to such a thing with rage. The anger partly subsides to false amusement. What's more embarrassing; being stood with your Batman underwear on show while everyone laughs at you or with you?

After a good skeg (regional variations would have it known as 'scants' or 'debriefing'), many victims try - unsuccessfully - to exact revenge there and then. The skegger, of course, is expecting this. He's on his toes, darting away as the victim lurches uselessly for his waistband.

In point of fact, the best plan of action is to mentally catalogue the owing of one skegging and to exact revenge at a later date, some time in the future when least expected. As the Klingon proverb goes, 'Revenge is a dish best served cold'.

Many months may have passed, but when payback is finally extracted, the victim will instantly accept that they had it coming. They won't have a leg to stand on. (Due mostly to the fact that their pants will be around their ankles and so standing on one leg could only make for further embarrassment.)

Just as many sports have one widely-accepted finest moment etched into their history – Chris Hoy's sixth gold medal in cycling, Manchester United's injury time comeback in 1999, the Rumble in the Jungle, or Torvill and Dean's Bolero - the pinnacle of skegging will surely forever be the time when Daryl Allison humbled Craig McDonald in the St Mark's playground.

The waistband lowered in one seamless, beautiful move - think Federer's forehand in his pomp for an idea of the quality of this technique - and without further ado, the multi-coloured atrocity that were Craig's underpants were exposed for every one of his schoolmates to see. The execution was perfect, location ideal, trousers falling in as open and busy a space as the school boasted; the reaction everything an onlooker could want, an exquisite mix of earth-swallow-me embarrassment and incandescent, bubbling rage.

What will stay with me for the rest of my life about this one particular skeg is the fact that Craig walked straight to the headmaster's office to 'grass' - with Daryl following at his heels in a begging, pleading pile of humility. That will never leave me, for the simple, incredible fact that Craig inexplicably did so with his trousers still at ankle-height, toddling in an awkward pants-on-show shuffle.

To this day, it remains a mystery to all who witnessed it

quite why Craig decided to do this walk of shame, several hundred yards long, exposed as he was. Stumbling over his trousers and waddling like a penguin, perhaps his brain never kicked fully back into gear from that 'What's going on?' stage.

Several onlookers blew a funny fuse, guffawing so hard that eventually the laughter subsided to a painful gasp for air, as faces turned red. For some, there was a genuine worry that if Craig didn't put his pants away soon, they might actually die of laughter.

Although secondary school was truly one of the greatest experiences of my life - a real joyous time filled with hysterical memories such as Skeg-gate - it was also a terrifying ordeal which left your nerves constantly on edge. I spent much of the time petrified, like the demented last survivor in a slasher flick, inexplicably stepping down into the basement with nothing but a lit match in a power cut.

In addition to the ever-present threat of pants exposés, there were an untold number of other humiliating pitfalls lurking around every corner.

Chief among our concerns was 'the banking', a steep hill covered in grass. Long before I even went to St Mark's, older kids were handing out wide-eyed warnings about keeping well away from the banking for the whole of first year. A long-held tradition dictated that S1s were to be flung mercilessly down the hill by senior pupils, often total strangers, as a sort of (very) informal induction.

Wee guys in their fledgling weeks of secondary education would be peacefully making their way from the bus drop-off to Regi. class when some bigger, stronger boys would suddenly grab hold and send them sailing through the air to the grass some ten feet below. Some of us were forewarned and forearmed, keeping clear of the area near the banking or making our way past cautiously. Others knew nothing of the tradition and discovered it only as they landed agonisingly on the corner of a hardback book poking through their school bag, after flying in bemused freefall for several seconds.

It hurt like hell, but somehow the tradition continued, banking victims one day becoming banking bullies and needlessly passing the torment on to their juniors. Psychologists would have a field day, as the abused became abusers.

Other reasons to be on edge or suffer pain in those torturous school days were infinitesimal. Traditions were many and new games often sprung up then disappeared after some weeks of fervent play.

One favourite was 'Trippy Uppy'. This downright idiotic game was basically a rudimentary Judo, where without warning, a trusted 'mate' would send you flying to the deck. Variants included:

1) quickly approaching someone side-on, sticking your right leg behind theirs and pushing their body backwards over your leg.

2) silently sneaking up behind someone as they walked and clipping their backwards foot as it stepped – tangling it with their standing leg and sending them crashing to the ground with forward momentum, or into a demented, involuntary goosestep.

3) crouching on all fours directly behind some unsuspecting victim then having your mate push them backwards over your hunched body.

Each method as stupid and painful as the last. As with the banking – and so many of our hurt-inflicting rituals – you hated having it done to you but happily did it to others, all to be part of the gang.

So much of this supposed fun involved hurting each other as much as possible. When we became bored of a game of football, it would be seamlessly adapted into a game of 'Hacky'.

This was an every-man-for-himself style game where the aim was to maintain possession of the ball while every other player tried to 'hack' you.

In stark contrast to actual football, just about every form of contact was permitted. In hindsight, it's a wonder that anyone voluntarily took the ball – perhaps it would just land at your feet and stay there amidst the ensuing melee, while your classmates took it in turns to trip your ankles, kick your shins, elbow your sides and just full-on batter fuck out of you.

Often the ball would leave your feet and the hammering would continue ceaselessly until someone was spotted making off in the opposite direction in control of the ball, trying in vain to get as far away as humanly possible from the violence.

Likewise, 'Peggy' involved nutmegging a friend with a crushed soda can then beating the shit out of them, all as some sick punishment for daring to let a lump of aluminium pass unknowingly between their feet.

Sometimes this violence was not dressed up in the form of the game. It would simply be dished out for no reason whatsoever, a punch to the stomach when someone was least expecting it. At times this would be a daily occurrence – pupils getting gut-punched whilst walking the halls, simply for being in the wrong place at the wrong time.

Worse still was the 'Chyna', where one would sneak up behind a mate and bless their bollocks with the gift of an uppercut. The name Chyna came from a female wrestler of the same name who was really only known for cutting about dishing out low blows.

What a sight it was to see a room full of schoolboys squeezing their legs together because someone had started a round of Chynas, everyone looking every inch like they had shat themselves, trying desperately to preserve their chances of one day continuing the family name.

The pain from a 'Titty Twister' or 'Nipple Crusher' would last for mere hours at a time, as would that of a dead leg - a result of some sod forcibly ramming his knee into the side of a muscle. In comparison to the agony which followed every visit of the school nurse, dead legs and crushed nipples were harmless, totally bearable.

My own physical hurt through secondary school was never more torturous than in the fortnight after getting my TB jag administered by said school nurse. Excruciatingly painful. Exponentially worse with every fresh punch. That every other boy in my year was going through the same living hell made the sufferance no easier.

Eventually, by about the tenth time that the area had been thumped, I started to accept the idea that I didn't really need feeling in my right arm and that with enough practice, I could adapt and learn to write with my other hand *.

In kinder walks of life, surely none of this hurt was inflicted; and if it was then were birthdays not the one event which would permit some brief reprieve from the onslaught? Not in our school. The misery of birthdays worsened with each year thanks to the tradition of 'dumps', where the celebrant would be gifted a punch/knee to the back for every year they had survived.

Nothing says 'Happy birthday!' like a mad horde of your peers chasing you around the school ground to thump you black and blue.

Senselessly, pupils would also injure *themselves* in the name of amusement. I'm confident that at every single state school across Scotland, children gave themselves 99-ers. Literally everyone I know who went to school in the late nineties and early noughties remembers 99-ers.

The 99-er was an utterly bizarre ritual that involved giving yourself a scab on the back of your hand. Using a rubber, ruler or simply your fingernail, you would scratch

* An altogether different schoolboy trauma concerning the school nurse arose with the long-surviving rumour that on your first visit, she asked you to drop trousers, placed a cold spoon against your scrotum and made you cough. Sheer panic, thankfully unfounded, at the very thought.

at the back of your hand as intensely and quickly as possible, counting from one to ninety-nine as you did so, a group of classmates watching and egging you on.

The area would first go white, then pink, eventually turning a tormented red colour before finally gushing with blood during the high eighties and nineties of your count.

Pride won from this could be enjoyed for days thanks to the resulting scab. The showing off of 99-er scars and the very fact that this could win absolute playground respect surely summarises how monstrously stupid childhood can be.

God only knows where this originated from. The fad would disappear for any number of reasons – a teacher lecturing us on infection, the rumour that you could get skin cancer from it – and start again for no reason other than the teacher running five minutes late for class. We had to fill the time somehow, and it may involve more pain.

P.E. periods would begin and end with 'ice burns'. As we changed into – and later out of – our P.E. kit, guys would produce deodorant cans from their kit bags and so the challenge would begin. Who was man enough to spray a full aerosol point-blank on the back of their hand or other random body part? The concentrated blast would sting like hell so the longer you could face the pain, the cooler you were.

Again, there seemed to be no rhyme or reason behind this other than it being sore for those involved and hilarious for everyone else.

One boy was physically sick and had to sit out that day's lesson after spraying whatever naff odour of Lynx was in vogue all over his testicles. One can only imagine the excruciating and immense discomfort he faced for days to come. At least his balls smelled like chocolate.

Humiliating and wounding your fellow academy comrades was not limited to physical hurt. At one point the popular sport was ripping the breast pockets off each other's shirts.

Obviously, it was open season on unbranded gear which had been bought cheaply from Asda or Tesco. The tearing of branded shirts won the most kudos.

Damaging Ben Sherman shirts was often seen to be a step too far. These expensive tokens of pocket-ripping warfare could only be won by the toughest and meanest guys with whom no one would dare argue.

Eventually, as with most of these games, the school authorities started threatening to suspend people. This almost certainly came about as a result of the poor soul who got his entire shirt ripped during first period.

Needless to say, vandalism of clothes was not by any means limited to the destruction of those useless pockets.

Kids would pinch bits of chalk from teachers in order to scrape big, white lines across their mates' clothes. If done discreetly, the only limit to what adorned the back of someone's jumper was your imagination.

I have seen mates traverse the 'admin corridor' – home to the offices of the administrative staff as well as the depute heads and head teacher – of St Mark's, blissfully unaware that an ejaculating phallus decorated their uniform. Senior staff would erupt at the victim until frustratedly realising their rage was misplaced; clearly no one would voluntarily walk the school halls adorned in a self-inflicted, chalky orgasm. Angry eyes would scan the corridor for the perpetrators, finding nothing but a corridor full of young boys pointing and laughing.

In lieu of chalk, anything one could get their hands on would suffice. A marker pen stain on a white Helly Hansen jacket was the cause of more than one playground fight.

The decision to stock the little bottles of Irn-Bru worth twenty-five pence in the tuck shop proved catastrophic for many a school jacket. Kids would bite through the bottom of the plastic on sealed bottles, shake like mad and then spray the sticky orange drink through the hole and on to any innocents within a ten yard radius.

How the 'I'm gonnae tell ma maw' response fared would depend on the craziness of the vandal in question. Decent kids threatened with the introduction of the victim's mother would tremble at the very thought and would usually become overly apologetic, taking over the efforts to clean said mark. The hard men of the playground would hit back with 'On ye go then'. The bluff had been called, and there would suddenly be an invisible line drawn under the notion of grassing.

Some innovative vandal once took the decoration of uniforms to new extremes by going to the length of bringing in toothpaste and 'pasting' fellow pupils. That was beyond the pale, it was generally agreed.

New clothes always provoked a response from classmates. Worst of all, buying trainers was simply more hassle than it was worth. The 'christening' of box-fresh footwear, where mates would stomp dirty marks all over your shoes, was a rite of passage which every pupil had to endure. Brand new shoes would be filthy by day two. Those fortunate families who could afford to buy Nike Airs with the pop-able bubbles on the inner heel made the mistake of doing so only once; no new Nike survived a day without being burst open.

Clothes were not only fair game for vandalism, but for mockery and outright bullying. Just some of the brands which won respect or admiration were Sweater Shop, Joe Bloggs, Pringle, Adidas, Russel Athletic, Le Coq Sportif and Lacoste.

Kappa, Ellesse and Sergio Tacchini were all highly fashionable for a short time. Decent makes which would usually attract no comment were things like Umbro, Mizuno, Puma and Reebok.

Outright losers included Gola, Asics, Cica and Donnay. Any item of clothing deemed unacceptable was branded 'a shiter'.

Example: 'That jumper is an absolute shiter, mate. Where did you get it, Poundland?'

There really was nothing more soul-destroying than your mother coming back from the shops on a Saturday with some toxic-brand clobber for the new term.

'Hi-Tec, Mum?! I can't go into school wearing Hi-Tec, are you having a bloody laugh?!'

I once witnessed a boy being sent home from school because he was wearing new Bull Boy shiters *.

It was never clear whether he was allowed to go home in order to save him from further bullying from his fellow pupils or because of the absolute disgust the teacher had for his choice of footwear; but the fact that it was more likely to be the latter says everything you need to know about the toxicity of the brand.

Debate still rages as to whether two stripes or four stripes were more embarrassing. In an age when 'Three Stripes' were king, there was simply nothing worse than having the wrong number of stripes on your trackies. Two stripes were deemed poor, the accusation usually that the family were so impoverished that they couldn't afford a third stripe. Four stripes were roundly slagged as a misguided attempt to be cool: trying to take the popularity of three stripes and go one better by adding a fourth.

One joker even strolled into school with trousers bearing *five* stripes one time. If there's any justice in the world, that kid was taken round back and given the Rodney King treatment by the Fashion Police.

GAP clothes were also a no-go, for the simple reason that 'GAP' became known around the playground as an

* Possibly the shortest-lived make of footwear ever, Bull Boy shoes briefly found fame as 'the trainers advertised by Alan Hansen and Gareth Southgate'. These were shoes of the same calibre as those endorsed by Drederick Tatum ('I have been given lots of money to endorse these butt ugly shoes'.) The advert jingle went: 'Bull Boy shoes is what you need, get the power on your feet!' Sadly, Bull Boy shoes long ago went the way of the Tamagotchi. Good night, sweet prince.

acronym for 'Gay and Proud'.

While Burberry sportswear is now the fashion of choice solely of smackheads, there was a brief period in the late nineties when it made for the coolest item of clothing on the planet: the baseball cap.

Seemingly blind to how utterly hideous they looked, loads of folk in our first year class back in 1998 sported these horrible hats, cream with a black, white and red checked pattern. Knowing nothing of the pattern's middle class history, spotty-faced teenagers wore these caps with pride. Not possessing this latest fad, I was so jealous of anyone who owned one, unable to view the accessory objectively and see how fucking ridiculous they looked.

I pleaded with my mum to take me shopping for a Burberry cap. I point blank needed one. We ended up in the Burberry shop in Glasgow; a gleaming, spotless store, all white marble and shining chandeliers with no coat or scarf priced cheaper than £100. My poor mother was practically laughed out of the store by the snotty-nosed saleswoman after enquiring if they stocked baseball caps *.

Clothes vandalism, fashion-related bullying and brand peer pressure, all just part of secondary school.

Yet more horridness was evident in the fact that the penning of arms and faces often came in to vogue. Some poor sod would inevitably end up sitting through a wild-eyed lecture from an R.E. teacher about the fact that they had a drawing of an anatomically-correct vagina - dripping wet and hairier than Chewbacca's armpit – etched upon their face in permanent marker which point-blank refused to wash off.

In a similarly cruel vein, I remember taking a packet of Blu Tack, breaking it into more than a hundred tiny pieces

* This was not the last time I embarrassed my mother in a Glasgow shop. She also remembers going into a music store on Sauchiehall Street to buy an item off my Christmas list, namely the CD *Hooray For Boobies* by the Bloodhound Gang. She eventually had to ask for assistance in finding it, all the while dreading the thought that I had made up an album title and put her up to it for a laugh.

and spending a whole English period with Alistair Sullivan throwing the bits into the hair of Laura, the oblivious girl at the desk in front. On later discovering as much, she and a friend spent all of lunch break picking the bits out, apparently with no end of pain, and it was more than a month before either of them spoke to us again.

There was also a ridiculous amount of psychological damage dished out. Life at school was a never-ending gauntlet of pranks and tricks that left you mentally exhausted; keeping abreast of the latest things that classmates were using to trip people up with was no mean task.

For instance, fellow pupils would lure you into joining the mysterious 'Pen fifteen' club by drip-feeding you tantalising titbits of information.

It's the cool new club – it's great once you're in it - the teachers don't know about it - and everybody is joining in.

This last revelation, of course, was the one that hooked you. Who needed hard facts about this club when you had just heard that not joining would effectively make you a social leper?

In their rush to join up, eager pupils would foolishly go along with the initiation to this supposed club: 'You have to write "pen one five" on the back of your hand'.

Teachers were never impressed to find stupid, unwitting pupils with 'PEN15' daubed in big bold letters on their person.

If a mate clued you in to the latest scam before someone tried to hustle you with it, you could live to fight another day.

Personal questions were a regular feature of our classroom discussions, inevitably centred around sex, sexy teachers, sexy pupils, or sexuality.

'Do you masturbate? My big brother says every guy does it...'

Again, with any luck, your pal would already have

briefed you on the latest question going round, so you weren't left flabbergasted when it was sprung upon you. With a little time to think, you could usually have something bordering on a reasonable answer ready, instead of just turning red and starting to sweat profusely.

That these quizzing sessions got increasingly personal the further we ventured into our school careers made the original 'Are you a V.L?' look so tame and impersonal that it wouldn't look out of place on a job application form.

'How many pubes have you got?' soon became the question everyone demanded an answer to. Was this really the sort of detail you were expected to know off-hand? Were you supposed to strip down and count there and then? And what on earth was a good answer: forty? Was that a reasonable amount? Far too high?! Laughably low?!

It was almost impossible to be asked as much and not turn red with embarrassment and indignation.

These questions would often be designed to trip you up or catch you out. When we were young, ignorant, and first growing used to our own burgeoning sexuality, nothing seemed funnier than the idea of someone being gay.

'Are you gay?' the question often went.

'No!'

'Really? There's nothing wrong with being gay'.

'I know, but I'm not'.

'Are you sure?'

'Yes, I'm straight'.

'It's okay to be gay. It just means 'happy'. Honestly, look it up in the dictionary, that's what it means'.

'Yeah, well, I'm still not gay'.

'You're not happy?'

'I am happy'.

'So you're gay?'

'No'.

'You are gay if you're happy! That's all it means. I'm gay, he's gay, we're all just happy. So are you gay?'

This would continue until you relented, never wanting to be the only one saying or doing something different from your classmates. Eventually you'd admit 'Yes, okay, I'm gay, but only meaning I'm ha...'

'Haha! You're gay! Did you all hear that, boys? He's just said he was gay! Poofter! Watch your backs, lads, watch your backs!'

Another way of entrapping someone in an admission of homosexuality (shock horror!) was pointing to their feet and making them look at the ground by quickly muttering 'You've dropped your gay card...'

There can't be a child of the era who didn't also, at one point, admit to having their own 'Personal Arse Licker'.

For a time, the popular scam was to dupe schoolmates with devious questions about members of their social circle.

'Is he your pal?'

'Yeah'.

'So he licks your bum then?'

'Eh, what?! No! Where did you get that from?'

'That's what "PAL" means! "Personal Arse Licker". You just admitted that he's your PAL'.

'Yeah, I didn't mean like that though! He's just my friend'.

'Aye. Your friend who licks your arsehole for you...'

Years on, kids of the nineties, now in their twenties and thirties, need to be careful who they discuss their friendships around. The temptation to chime in at mention of the word 'Pal' with 'What, your personal arse licker?' is still just too strong for some.

Another scam to make your pal (small P) look like a tit was to insist that you could make them taste salt using nothing but their imagination.

'Tilt your head back... That's it. Now close your eyes, and pretend you're holding a salt shaker. If you pretend to shake it onto your tongue, you get the taste of salt in your mouth. It's amazing!'

Eventually they would bemoan that nothing was happening, to which you'd reply:

'I know, but you've just done a brilliant impression of sucking a guy off…'

Yet another good dodge was to ask friends what the capital of Thailand was. Their reply – 'Bangkok' – gave you carte blanche to thump them in the groin.

Or asking 'Did you get that letter I sent?'

'No'.

'That's because I forgot to stamp it!' – said with a smirk and a hard stamp on their foot.

If all that wasn't enough, you could raise a cheap laugh by getting your mate to spell 'ICUP' aloud, or entrap your buddies in an admission of self-pleasuring, by asking them to put an index finger in either side of their mouth, pull their cheeks apart and shout 'I'm a banker! I'm a banker!'

It was all utterly exhausting.

Needless to say, St Mark's had a school counsellor. Hers must have been a revolving door, her office a line of persecuted wee guys questioning their sexuality, enquiring as to how many pubic hairs a fourteen year old boy should have, begging her for some second-hand Adidas gear, or asking if she knew how to get marker pen out of a white Helly Hansen jacket.

XVII: THE FULL MONTY
'I saw you at the weekend, sir!'

Blurring that classic line between comedy and tragedy, Mr. Montgomery's time spent cheerily teaching our unruly class and his subsequent fall from grace some years later both delights and saddens me.

A short, jolly man with white hair and a broad range of guff 'dad' ties, Monty taught us Business Management and was probably best known as the man who enthusiastically ran the SMASH (St Mark's After School Homework) Club.

The two strongest memories I have of Business class demonstrate well the two sides of 'wee Bobby', as he was affectionately known.

Usually he was to be found in good spirits, heartily nattering away to pupils in the corridor between periods, whistling as he walked from class to class, making casual conversation with his classes during lessons. Periods in Business with Mr. Montgomery, whilst not always riveting, were generally fun.

The best time I ever had in his class was as summer approached, the last term of the year drawing in to a close. Divided into teams, we were each group to create a business, advertise it and run our commercial enterprise on school grounds.

I and two other lads made our own car wash company, informed every teacher of our services, and spent the next few days basking in glorious sunshine, washing cars and making serious cash. Best of all, we were allowed to divide and keep whatever profit we made.

My mum was a tad concerned at how I had suddenly come into money, finding a wad of notes in my school trouser pockets. I grabbed them off her with an 'I was looking for those – thanks, doll!' and left her stewing for a few more days, before eventually telling her about the business and reassuring her that I hadn't turned to a life of crime.

Our time in the car valet business is a lasting, happy memory I took from my school career and whilst maybe an oversimplification of business start-up, a lesson which will always stick with me.

Mr. Montgomery's other extreme was a mad, flaring temper. Like many teachers, wee Bobby had that unpredictable tendency to flip out and put the frighteners on any misbehaving kids. Classes soon learned to avoid these rare freak-outs.

Most teachers were fair game for 'bamming up', deliberately goading them to flip, with all the ensuing hilarity that that would bring. Not Mr. Montgomery. His worst mood swings were genuinely terrifying, and no one seemed eager to provoke him.

My enduring memory of this temper was one day that we were each given our own iMac to log in to in order to play a new business simulator. The game was a fairly basic sim – think a second-rate *Theme Park*, *Sim City*, *Football Manager* – which allowed you to start a business, budget, decide what stock to order, how to advertise and so on.

Naturally, it took a bit of explaining to get twenty-odd pupils up to speed with how the software worked. The first fifteen minutes or so of the lesson were spent going over the basics. At that, we were left to log on to our machines and start our own virtual career in retail.

Every one of us happily stuck our headphones on and started clicking away. Just moments later, Gordon Butler uttered that immortal line which he would soon come to so badly regret. Subconsciously and unwittingly shouting over the noise of his headphones with all the volume of a pilot issuing mayday cries from a nose-diving bomber, he turned to his friend and asked 'I wisnae listening, whit the FUCK are we meant to be doin' here?!'

The book which flew across the room and missed Gordon's head 'by a bawhair' sent plaster crumbling from the wall that it struck. Monty's incandescent shouting was indecipherable, but as every head in the room spun round in shock, Gordon got the gist. Bobby pointed furiously, spitting like some riled ape, and Gordon slunk quietly out the classroom door. He spent the afternoon in the corridor, and I spent the rest of the period just barely able to concentrate on my simulated business between fits of quiet laughter.

Fully some eight years after leaving school, I logged on to the internet and my Facebook feed one morning to be struck with Mr. Montgomery's photo. I did a double take, tried to quickly reconcile why on earth a teacher I hadn't seen in almost a decade was on my news feed, then slowly read the headline of the attached article: 'Teacher suspended over sex website claims'.

I was so shocked that my eyes actually popped out of my head and my jaw literally hit the floor. I looked like the horny, whistling wolf in a Tex Avery cartoon. My funny fuse blew; here was something so hilarious that the response went beyond laughter. Physically, my body didn't know what to do. It was like a gut punch to the stomach.

A former teacher of mine had been suspended. For misconduct. OF A SEXUAL NATURE!

I have a theory that every school has at least one

teacher embroiled in rumours of a 'misconduct' scandal. Sometimes it might be something as sinister as talk of an affair with a pupil and corridor whispers of what a terrible 'nonce' the teacher is – other times it might be that someone saw two teachers having it off in a supplies cupboard, or a pupil swearing on their mum's life that they know a guy who knows a guy who knows a doctor who insists that Mr. Smith had to be rushed to A&E at the weekend to get a potato removed from his arse. None of it had to be true, it just had to be believable and above all else, funny.

And here was ours. Confirmed, there in print in that bastion of truth that is *The Sun* for all to see.

In a nutshell, it transpired that poor Bobby liked meeting strangers in the car parks of his hometown of Seaville in order to stick his bits in them in the confines of their vehicle. Someone had alerted *The Sun* to the fact that a teacher at our Catholic school not only enjoyed doing so, but had a profile on dogging.co.uk which listed 'cyber sex', 'webcam fun' and 'erotic emails' among his interests. There was even a picture of him wearing nothing but his boxers, with his 'wee Bobby' poking out the side of said briefs. Before long, all of this was out there as a news story to be shared on social media sites with easily amused goons like me.

My body might be that of an adult, but at the controls sits a child. It was all I could do not to laugh, with no regard whatsoever for the tragedy of the circumstances.

Browsing the 'net before heading off later that day to my responsible, full-time job, I sat there in my pyjamas and very quickly regressed to being twelve years old, half my actual age at the time. I was so quickly transported back to school and couldn't help but imagine the indescribable fun we could have had with that revelation in a classroom.

What excited chatter would shriek around the playground that break-time. How many brilliant ways the topic could be inappropriately broached with teachers desperately trying to change tack. What sort of monumental, emergency assembly the incident would ultimately lead to.

Eventually, much later, I came to realise that I actually had a lot of sympathy for the guy. Frankly, if you and your partner want to cram into the back of a Renault Clio with some other consenting adults for a shift of the gear stick and a poke at an exhaust pipe, all power to you.

However, after reading the article at least three times, still in shock and literally shaking with uncontrollable laughter – way, way ahead of the point at which I would stop, take stock of the situation and actually feel sorry for a decent guy suspended for harmless activities he got up to in his own time – I posted a link to the article to my Facebook friends and opened the floor to suggestions: In light of this news, what else could his SMASH (St Mark's After School Homework) Club stand for? The resulting hundreds of suggestions made for one of the best laughs I have ever had, and very nearly made me late for work. Below are some of my favourites:

Sir Makes A Sexual Howler
Seaville Monty, A Sexual Heathen
Stupid Man And Shattered Homelife
Sorry, Monty, Am Shunning Homework
Sir Meets Adventurous Shaggers Hush-Hush
Stop Molesting Anonymous Strangers, Horrible
Shagger Monty Angers School Headteacher
Shall Mount At Hotspot
St Mark's After School Homewreckers Club
Sleazy Male After Slutty Hos
See Me, Am Sordid & Homeless
Slag Monty About Sexual Hi-jinks
Sir, My Ass Seriously Hurts
Seldom Male Agoraphobic Shaggers Here...

Schoolteacher's Misery and Suicide Hell
Shag My Arse So Hard
Spunky Meriva A Seller's Horror
Shall Meet At Sir's House??
St Mark's Academy Suspends Horndog
Sordid Monty Assfucks Skoda Hotty!
See Me, Ah Shag Hondas!
Some May Attend Sexual Healthclinic
Students Marvel As Sir Hamshanks
Secretly, Monty A Sexual Hedonist
Sir's Medically-Assisted Stranger Hankypanky
So, My Adolescence Sullied, Horrendously
Sex Meetups At Seaville Harbour
Shunning Monty Around School Hallways
See Me After School, Horny
So, Monty: Ashamed, Stupid Head?
Subarus May Arouse Sir's Horniness
Sun Makes Angry Seaville Housewife
School May Alter Staff Hiring
Stripped Man Annihilates Subaru's Handbrake
Seatbelts May Affect Sir's Handjob
Sometimes Masturbating's A Safer Hobby
Seaville Man Arrested Shining Headlights
Suspension Modified After Shagger's Holiday
Shadowy Masturbator Alarms Seaville Housewives
Seat, Mazda, Alfa... Sir's Horny!
Several Motors All Sullied Horrendously
Sir's Mankini's Anal Stains, Horrific
Suspended Monty Auctioning Secondhand Honda
Sir Misuses A School Hewlett-Packard
Stolen Moments At Seaville Harbour
Scalextric Miniatures Arousing Sir's Horniness
Slimy Man Adores Sexy Housewives
Sexy Monty Approaches Stranger's Hyundai...

XVIII: UP IN THE SKY
*'Will you turn that crap down to a dull roar?!
I can't hear myself thinking!'*

The 1990s was a time of great quality music, with culturally important bands and releases throughout the years. However, as a child growing up in the decade, these defining moments of artistic significance passed me by.

I was largely ignorant of it all: Nirvana, Pearl Jam, Pixies, and the rise of grunge; Britpop and the battle of Blur vs. Oasis, or indeed classic albums like The Stone Roses' self-titled and Radiohead's *OK Computer*; wholly new genres like electronica, hip-hop and rap exploding into the mainstream limelight. Then? Not on my radar.

Music was not a serious interest as a child, not something to be passionate about or explore with any real effort. Songs were introduced to you via means such as Saturday morning television, school parties (who can forget Black Lace's *Superman* with accompanying dance moves?), magazines like *Smash Hits*, chart-toppers on the radio, and compilation cassettes bought from Woolworths or Our Price (the *Now That's What I Call Music!* series in particular). Later, the unwieldy and impractical CD Walkman came into vogue.

At ice skating parties, kids fell in love with songs like *Ecuador* by Sash and N Trance's *Set You Free*. A tape of *Now! 95* introduced me to tunes such as *'74-'75* by The Connells, The Outhere Brothers' *Boom Boom Boom* and *Search For The Hero* by M People.

Boy bands – Boyzone, 911, East 17, Backstreet Boys, Take That – would be foisted upon wee boys against their will thanks to sisters and female friends.

We had them all trumped though, with the Spice Girls held up as the absolute pinnacle of musical brilliance by every boy under the age of fourteen. Everyone had their favourite (mine was Ginger Spice). No bedroom was complete without a poster. Our burgeoning sexuality had such a say in our young lives that we even tolerated their music and could reel off the names of their best songs.

Novelty songs and catchy hits always fared well. Some of the biggest songs of the time included *MMMbop* by Hanson, *Macarena* by Los del Rio, *Cotton Eye Joe* by Rednex, Aqua's *Barbie Girl*, *Mambo No. 5* by Lou Bega, the *Mr. Blobby* song, *Let's Get Ready To Rumble* by PJ & Duncan and *Spaceman* by Babylon Zoo.

We would make our own compilations using tape-to-tape recorders. Few of the songs featured on those home-made collections have survived into the modern-day music libraries of nineties' kids. Scant few of our childhood songs are still viewed with credibility: only the odd nostalgic survivor like Coolio's *Gangsta's Paradise*, *Bitter Sweet Symphony* by The Verve, Supergrass' *Alright* and *You Get What You Give* by the New Radicals could be trotted out at today's parties with any sort of dignity.

Only towards the end of the decade did I start to carve out my own taste in music, discovering Nirvana and then nu-metal such as Linkin Park, Limp Bizkit and Korn. Festivals started to garner my attention: T In The Park, Gig On The Green, Reading & Leeds, with dreams in my early teens of seeing bands like Green Day, Blink-182 and

Foo Fighters live.

The first festival I went to had acts like Alien Ant Farm, Staind and Papa Roach. I was in heaven, in awe of these flash-in-the-pan bands that would soon be playing dive bars with pishy carpets and glory holes in the restrooms.

There, the festival addiction was born, my teenage years then spent scrounging together enough cash to hit another couple of events each summer.

It was an eye-opening time, festivals introducing me to a mad, alternative world full of fun and misadventures.

There was the time I got so blind drunk at one festival that I lost my passport in the massive camping fields, only for someone to find it and recognise me in the melee of seventy thousand other pissheads.

The guy at Leeds Festival who climbed down into a toilet and perched on the metal beams running above the enormous pit of faeces, all so he could jump out on the next person to enter the little cubicle and shout 'POP UP PIRATE! POP UP PIRATE!'

The night a gang of twenty or more of us crawled around the campsite on our hands and knees, sneaking up to groups of people round campfires then meowing like cats, provoking total bemusement all round and probably ruining at least one good trip.

Dozens of pals lining up outside a Portaloo in the dead of night to form a guard of honour, breaking into really enthusiastic applause and whooping the second the unsuspecting user stepped back out.

Space hopper races, free chips and deep-fried Mars bars blagged from food vendors, sneaking into the catering area to steal rolls for our barbecue, setting up a very successful campsite toll to charge punters to return to their tents, the karaoke attempt my pal Cat and I still haven't lived down... Summers spent living out of tents, making some of the craziest memories of my life. And sneaking alcohol into the arena; always sneaking alcohol into the arena.

One of the nuttiest stories from those days was told to me by a pal over a campsite beer one night, and involved a certain mega rock band who for legal reasons, will not be named. Suffice to say that they are smashing, pumpkins.

Jim — not his actual name, but it's been a long-held desire of mine to publish a story that necessitated a name change — has for many years had a job driving vans at one of the UK's major festivals each summer. I was, at first, surprised to learn this, not least because he looks about eleven years old, which last time I checked is not even old enough to own a provisional.

Bands arrive and get driven around the huge site by Jim. In return, he gets a free ticket and camping. I begrudge him this great reward for such easy labour; I or anyone else at the festival could quite easily perform this simple task in order to get a free ticket.

I'd probably struggle after the daily multipack of cheap cider I consume, but I'm pretty sure I could do it without too many fatalities.

So one time, Jim is happily driving this particular rock band around site, and is given the fairly major task of ferrying them to the stage for their headline performance in front of eighty thousand fans.

Having done so successfully - presumably navigating round a course of lost and drunk hippies along the way - Jim arrives backstage with the band in one piece. He smiles, switches the engine off, and there's a pregnant pause which would normally be punctuated by the band saying their 'Thank you's and stepping out.

Suddenly, band frontman Billy says to Jim: 'Eat this bit of toast'.

Jim, momentarily confused and fairly certain that 'What to do if a headline act offers you supper' wasn't covered in the short Dos and Don'ts speech which the festival representative gave the crew on Friday morning, manages to quickly regain composure. Flying solo without prior toast-based guidance from his representative, he swiftly thinks on his feet and replies: 'No, thank you'.

Strangely persistent, Billy says again: 'Eat this bit of toast'.

Jim replies: 'No thank you, I'm not hungry'.

There's a shift in the mood of the van. Suddenly there's a tension. Billy seems offended, then irately and with deadly seriousness utters the immortal line: 'Eat this bit of toast or we are not going on stage'.

And with that, Jim accepts the toast and forces himself to eat it. He bravely shoulders the responsibility and refuses to disappoint eighty thousand anxious fans, consuming the toasted bread like an absolute hero. The band step out and head for the stage.

Jim is left in the driver's seat, alone and a little upset, wiping the unsolicited crumbs from his chin. Privately, he knows that his action and his action alone is responsible for the headliners taking to the stage. The band went on to play a hits-packed set to rave reviews that night, trumpeted as one of the highlights of the weekend. Jim saved the festival.

For legal reasons, I should probably add that this story may have been embellished, misremembered, or flat-out made up, but this is exactly how it was relayed to me and I love the thought that it's true; so let's just say that it is.

All of this passport-losing, Mars-frying, poo-applauding, toast-eating madness was preceded by my first ever festival away from home, camping and all. And that was the scene of the wildest and most horrific incident of all.

I was only fifteen, and my parents were incredibly against the whole idea.

'You want to do what?!'

'Get myself down to Donington and camp at the festival for a few days'.

'Absolutely no way! On your own? It's too dangerous, son'.

'I wouldn't be going on my own! My pal wants to go, too'.

'Which pal?'

'Ach, you don't know him…'

'Oh, that's great! You're fifteen and you want to go the two hundred miles or whatever down to Donington for a few days, and we've to let you do this in the company of some boy we've never met? Dream on, Graeme'.

'His name's Darren, he's a… fun guy'.

The word 'fun' passed my lips after I caught myself going to say 'good' and then, instead, 'nice'. This was on a knife-edge. I had to keep track of all the threads I was weaving in order to pull this off; it was no time for lies. I barely knew Daz, and the only time I had really spent in his company had involved ordering £50 of takeaway food to his neighbour's house and watching with great amusement through his letterbox as it arrived, four of us running around his neighbourhood in our boxers at two in the morning, and throwing eggs through an open kitchen window.

All the makings of a perfect friend, in my estimation, but nothing there that would help win over Mum and Dad, and certainly nothing that could be described as 'good' or 'nice'. 'Fun' seemed about right.

Eventually, my parents relented, not due to any one argument I made but rather down to a *Simpsons*-style 'Will you take us to Mount Splashmore?!' tactic of relentless nagging.

It was left to Darren and I, teenage delinquents that we were, to sort our whole weekend, tickets, travel, tents and all. I guess it was a sort of 'sink or swim' approach to parenting – they disagreed with the whole thing in principle, so handed me the opportunity to go off and prove them right or prove them wrong.

'Our first option', I explained to Daz, after ten whole minutes of searching for Donington on a map of the UK, 'is that we fly directly into East Midlands Airport. It's literally a mile from the festival site. The flight will take less than an hour, all told'.

'Brilliant! Let's do that'.

'The only thing is, it'll cost £70 each'.

'Oh...'

'There is an alternative'.

'And what does that cost?'

'£20 each'.

'We'll do that then'.

The cheaper alternative was the Hell on wheels that is the Megabus: an innovative service that brings the prison experience to you for as little as £1 a journey.

Hop on and sample the misery of confinement in a hot, cramped disgrace to public transport, only marginally better than the images we've all seen of poor people in rural India sitting on bus roofs. Spend an hour on the bus for every pound you save on flights!

After just an hour on this moving toilet, I was a husk of a man, worn down to the point that if someone had offered me a means of transporting straight to the site at a cost of £50 (the saving we had made by foolishly not flying), I would have paid it twice over.

Once we arrived in Nottingham, the only obstacles between us and having a roof over our heads were 1) a bus from Nottingham city centre out to the site, 2) a three mile walk to the campsite, gear and all, with various checkpoints in between and 3) constructing our tent.

I take solace in the fact that there are probably still people out there who cheerily reminisce about our attempts to build a tent. Having arrived as the sun was setting, just as the rain clouds started to move across the darkening sky, we were surrounded by campers happily chilling round their campfires, in the space between their successfully erected tents.

Like a Chuckle Brothers' performance piece, we delighted onlookers with a slapstick routine – whacking each other inadvertently with poles, failing miserably to work out what was the right way round and what was inside-out, aborting several wonky-looking attempts and just generally imbuing the campsite with a bit of all-round 'To me! To you!'

Tent eventually erected, we stupidly started our way through a twenty-four can box of Tennent's Lager which would be polished off come the end of the three nights. While this would now scarcely be enough to last me alone on a festival weekend, it was more than enough for two wet-behind-the-ears teenagers on their first jolly away from home. Downing three or four cans a man each night, we would get loaded up with alcohol after the headliner had rounded off another day and get into mischief.

We were, as our friends back home would say, 'Wan Can Dans'.

So with festivities finished on the Sunday night - the two of us having spent three days on the sauce - we found ourselves drunk and deciding that the dodgems were a great idea. Next to the campsite there was a small fairground where inebriated idiots like us could willingly part with what remained in our wallets.

We flew round the ride absolutely giddy, giggling away like a pair of wee girls having a sleepover. There was an old guy, who must have easily been in his sixties, in an even worse state than us riding one of the cars; so drunk that he was going round the track the wrong way, oblivious. This seemed like the funniest thing in the world at that precise moment, and so we made it our mission to smash into him at top speed on every circuit we made of the ride. Wailing with laughter, we battered him with head-on collision after head-on collision, the poor bugger so dazed that he didn't even understand what was going on.

We practically fell out of the ride, staggering away from the dodgem cart on a high of alcohol and laughter. I put my arm round Daz and we started to stumble on, walking the aimless walk of the drunk, with our arms around each other's necks.

It was then that Daz stopped dead, suddenly grabbing his stomach with his free hand.

'What?' I chuckled.

I took one look at him, and realised something serious was going on.

'Ohhhhhhhhhhhh', he moaned.

'What is it?!'

'I don't feel so good, mate'.

'Why, what's wrong?' I asked, momentarily sobering up. 'Was it the crashing?'

'No it's... my stomach'.

Don't drink and drive, they say. Apparently dodgems and lager don't make for happy bedfellows where the innards of teenagers are concerned.

'Oh right', I said, astutely taking 'my stomach' to mean 'my arse'.

'I need...'

'I know, mate, we'll get you to a bog'. I looked all round, scanning the horizon for the nearest 'TOILETS' sign.

'No'.

'No? What do you mean, "No"?'

'I'm not going to make it'.

And at that, he lopped off into the darkness, running round to the back of the dodgems ride and disappearing into the night.

I stood with my mouth agape.

I supposed all I could do was wait, assuming that he would eventually reappear and come back to where he had left me.

I waited for what must have been fifteen minutes, watching my fellow revelers in a drunken stupour. In fact, the longer I stood, the more drunk I felt, eventually breaking into that shaky, classic pose where my left leg stood stock still on the spot but my right went back, forward, back, forward...

I had almost forgotten about Daz's desperate plight by the time he reappeared, looking white but happier, carrying something by his side.

'Well, how did you get on?' I asked cheerily.

'Aye, mate, that's better'.

I could hear the relief in his voice.

'Where did you go?'

'In a bag', he answered, taking my use of the word 'go' a little literally.

'I meant where did you... What, you actually went in a bag?'

'Yes'.

There was an awkward pause, in which both of our eyes looked downwards.

'In *that* bag?' I shrieked, pointing towards the carrier bag he was holding.

'Yes'.

I thought about it, then laughed. I hadn't known Daz long, but already I knew what a prankster he was. He had caught me out a few times with his claims, and left me looking like a right tit amongst our pals each time. He liked a laugh and a jape, and he could deadpan as well as anyone I had ever met.

'Bollocks'.

'What? Honest'.

In an open field big enough to hold eighty thousand festival goers, with hundreds if not thousands of Portaloos, there was absolutely no way that someone would be stupid enough to shit in a carrier bag, far less proceed to carry it around with them after the event.

Swing and a miss. It was too obvious.

'No way'.

'G, I promise you, I shat in this bag', he said calmly, seeming a bit miffed that I would doubt the veracity of this bizarre claim.

'Alright, then. Prove it'.

He stretched out his arm and offered me the bag.

I instantly regretted my demand. I didn't for a minute think that there was a turd in this bag, but it was at least up for debate, and let's face it: how else could he prove it but hand me the bag?

I held it at arm's length, disbelieving but not taking a risk, all the same; much in the same way that if someone dressed in military gear handed you what looked like a toy gun, you might politely decline a game of Russian Roulette.

I sure as hell wasn't about to bring the contents of the bag to my nose for a sniff, so how else could I test his bold claim?

I considered the weight of the bag. It certainly felt like a credible weight. I began to wonder what he had in fact put in the bag if not the contents of his bowels. A thought struck me.

'So if I was to toss this bag into the distance, into the campsite, your turd would go flying through the air along with it?'

'Yes!' he exclaimed, starting to become irate.

I looked him in the eye, hard. What a joker!

'Fine'.

And with that, I launched the carrier bag and its contents into the night, absolutely certain that it did not contain Daz's dump; why on earth would he let me throw it if it did?

No way.

We were next to the campsite, separated from it by a large metal fence, and the bag went sailing, up in the sky, over the heads of the oblivious campers below. It was a great throw, and the wind caught the bag just right; it hung in the air for an inordinately long time.

The flight of the bag was oddly compelling. We watched it, illuminated in the night sky by the moon and by campsite floodlights, and while it glided through the air - still to reach the peak of its arc - I asked him one last time, knowing he now had no reason to tell me anything but the truth, and that I could this time take his answer at face value.

'What really was in that bag, Daz?'

'My shit'.

'...Fucking hell', I managed.

We ran, as fast as I have ever run whilst suffering the effects of alcohol. We ran until our legs could no longer carry us, ran not to any one place in particular, simply away from the tortured howls of anguish that came from the direction in which I had thrown a Tesco bag of my pal's shit.

With age, I've grown to realise that my parents were right about an awful lot of stuff they warned against or chastised about. In hindsight, perhaps their concerns about Darren and I going off to a festival alone were well-founded.

XIX: THE END OF THE INNOCENCE
'It'll all end in tears!'

There had been an unspoken awkwardness since my return from the old lady's bathroom. There was the slurping of tea and the chinking of china, but not a lot any of us could say.

I was glad when the breakdown service finally arrived and we could leave, thanking her once again for her hospitality. She waved us off from her front door, and I firmly hoped I would never have to see her again.

Very soon, the feeling would be mutual. She would certainly be incredibly thankful to never have to smell me again, once the odour had eventually cleared in about a fortnight or so.

That was the poo de resistance of what went down as the worst Johnston family holiday ever. Having stayed in Dungloe, where we had previously spent many happy holidays (we started visiting in 1997 and would eventually buy a family holiday home there in 2005), our visit to the County Donegal village had on this occasion seen us lurch from one calamity to another.

The unreliability of our metallic green Vauxhall Vectra had been a key feature of a disastrous week in which we had already suffered an expensive car breakdown and rescue, in addition to my pulling a thigh muscle on a walk on which we got lost and the whole family coming down with flu-like symptoms.

By now, this latest setback felt like mere routine, part of the 'Holiday from Hell' itinerary.

'At 11 AM, guests can enjoy several hours of random vehicle failure in the middle of nowhere. Then join your rep "Paedo Dave" by the pool at 4 PM for kiddies' water polo - watch out for the floating tampons!'

I'm delighted to report that the diarrhea continued for the remainder of the holiday. When it transpired that our car was, basically, fucked, this meant I had to do a journey across Ireland to reach Dublin airport - and the flight that was our alternate means of getting home - in the back of a roasting hot rental car whilst holding in a wet fart for four hours. Successfully, I might add – I left a fair amount of 'excess baggage' in the airport toilets before boarding the flight home.

It's after just such an experience that the comforts of home do you good. After a long, arduous journey (via various lavatories), all I wanted to do was get home, unwind and forget about the worst week of my young life.

Unfortunately, what we were about to discover is that I am massively allergic to penicillin. The Irish doctor who I had visited days previously about my flu had put me on a course of antibiotics, and no sooner had we arrived home than the allergic reaction kicked in: an hour after I had noticed the first few red dots on my arms, my entire body was covered in a rash and my head had swollen up until I resembled the Elephant Man.

The astonished doctor I saw in A&E said he had never

seen a reaction like it. He actually giggled a little, the prick.

Thankfully, that has been the only bad trip to date to an area of the world that I now consider a home from home. Since the nineties, we have spent weeks or months of each year in the west of Ireland, growing to love its people and unique charm. As many families do, we found one corner of the globe we loved and continued to revisit it again and again throughout my childhood, such that Donegal is almost as much a part of my childhood as Scotland.

I had my first ever taste of alcohol there, after my mum's elderly relative had introduced my sister and I to her grandson and his friends. We met up with them that night to head into town and take in some of the entertainment on offer at the Mary From Dungloe festival (an annual event that was the inspiration for the Lovely Girls competition in *Father Ted*). We ended up watching a Queen tribute act play out of an arctic lorry while we each took glugs of cider from a three litre bottle. I had one of the best nights of my teenage years, followed by the roughest morning.

I attempted my first ever chat up line in a Dungloe pub. After seeing a blonde girl of roughly the same age as me during my summer holiday aged fourteen, I eventually decided after a week of lovestruck gawking to pluck up the courage and profess my admiration to her.

At the end of a bar lunch in which I had spied her once again, my family all got up to leave and as they headed for the door I told them I'd be out in just a minute. My best friend wasn't here to ask on my behalf, it seemed hers wasn't either; if I was going to do this, I would have to directly ask a girl out for the first time ever. I walked to her table as tall as I could manage, sat down with her and her family and tried my hand:

'I've seen you around here all week. I wondered if you wanted to go out a walk with me?'

'No'.

'Okay'.

After my meek reply, I got nothing further in response from the girl of my dreams. I didn't want to just up and leave, though. Her mum gave me a sympathetic look and traded a minute or so of stilted pity chat with me, before I slunk out the pub and spent the next week debating how my smooth offer of 'a walk' had somehow misfired. Having years earlier worked out 'Don't throw stones at your love interest's pet', my plan B had failed too. I felt like I was now back to square one, completely clueless as to how to finally blag myself a girl.

Dungloe was also where I saw my first ever fanny, though no thanks to my chat up lines. Another of mum's many Irish relations had a house outside of town with an extensive patch of land around it. One sunny summer day they held a small, off-the-cuff folk festival in their garden christened 'T In The Bog', with what seemed like half of the town in attendance. No doubt most of the crowd were related to my mum in some tenuous way.

As we all spread out on the hilly grass to enjoy an afternoon of local music, food and drink, I ended up with a fantastic view not only of the performers, but also up the dress of the twenty-something, knickerless stunner who had lay down on the lawn in front of me and spread her legs. It was like she had opened the Ark from *Indiana Jones and the Raiders of the Lost Ark*. My face nearly melted in shock at the sight of it. I kept my sunglasses on, didn't move for several hours and certainly didn't roll onto my back for fear of giving the game away. Magic.

The west coast of Ireland really is a special place, unlike anywhere else in the world, and not only because of its vaginas.

Drivers frequently block traffic as they stop their car in the middle of the street to shout across to a friend on the opposite pavement. People conduct five minute chats with a queue of inconvenienced cars at their tail, with never a cross word and only a series of lackadaisical waves to be shown for it.

The roads are emblazoned with letters in white paint proclaiming 'SLOW', then some yards later the word 'SLOWER'.

We once tried to visit the Slieve League cliffs in Donegal only to discover a small, hastily erected sign explaining that they were 'closed', due to foot and mouth disease among the local farm animals. Memories came flooding back of the episode of *Father Ted* where Dougal takes Jack to Fun Land instead of a walk to the cliffs, lying that they 'were closed'. Not that ridiculous after all!

The local sporting event of the year is the slow bike race, an annual tradition during the Mary From Dungloe festival where competitors try to get from the top of the extremely hilly main street to the bottom in the slowest time possible, feet never touching the ground, with hilarious consequences.

Timekeeping is a foreign concept. Nothing starts when advertised. We once went along to a fundraiser barbecue boasting quite possibly the latest start time for such a thing that the world has ever seen: 10 PM. Who starts a fucking barbecue at ten o'clock at night?!

To make matters worse, it was actually after 1 AM by the time burgers were eventually served!

Measurements are also alien. My mum remembers asking one of her elderly Irish relatives for the recipe to one of her home baking specialities only to be told to 'use a dod of this, add a handful of butter, heap some flour in…'

Similarly, forget asking for directions. It was all we could do not to laugh in an old Irishman's face after we asked him for help getting to a nearby village. It was one of our first holidays to the place and our local geography wasn't great yet. His various attempts at describing how to get there were foiled by our ignorance to any of his directions. Eventually he tried:

'Do you know the Gweedore Road?'

'Yes!' we enthused.

'Right, well it's not there…'

All in all, an agonising case of Elephantiasis and a severe bout of the runs - causing my arse to royally collapse in the middle of a stranger's house - were a small price to pay for dozens of happy holidays, some of the best experiences of my childhood and a beautiful home from home.

Besides – what goes around comes around. If I felt any guilt about abusing the hospitality of a sweet, old pensioner, karma was about to even things up, big time. I had shown that woman the perils of inviting guests into your humble commode; a lesson I would soon learn myself, in an afternoon that would slam shut the door on my childhood.

The 1990s were over. I had left school, arguably the last step in any young boy's life before joining the world of adulthood and all it entails.

With my perfect set of Standard Grades – all eight at 'Credit 1' – and five Highers, my mum and dad were no doubt thrilled that I decided to spend the next year or two dossing around, leaving the house only to toy with the odd menial job (one lasted for a week, enough to buy an Xbox, the other for two and a half days). I grew my hair, started playing guitar and spent most of my days pursuing my driving ambition – writing *Python*-style sketch comedy – with my equally lackadaisical friend, Peter.

To be fair to them, my parents were pretty cool about the whole thing, happy to put a roof over my head and support me while I at least gave this a try. Working life could wait.

But it did mean I was now a man of the house, expected to chip in with my fair share of housework and other household jobs, given the inordinate amount of time I was spending lazing around the place.

That meant things like loading and unloading the dishwasher (rarely), doing loads of washing (once) and cutting the grass (never).

Given my general uselessness in most other departments, it was the least I could do to agree to be home and helpful whenever my dad had cause to call workmen out to the house. And it was the visit of one such fellow, a roofer, which goes down as the darkest day of my teenage years.

Sure, it may sound like a non-event - bloke finds local handyman in *Yellow Pages*, phones, solicits business, pays cash - but I am not exaggerating when I say that short of tying me up and silencing my screams as he bummed me against a wall, a visit from the builder could not actually have been any worse.

In short, we had a leaky roof. A chap had been out one Saturday and after a sojourn up his ladders and an afternoon of banging noises - disturbing my mum from her *Dallas* DVDs - the guy declared he'd solved the problem. My old man squared up with him and off he went.

You can imagine our surprise when the leak continued, despite our being several hundred pounds in repairs poorer. Quick on the phone, my dad arranged a day and time for a second attempt, and as my only other plans that morning were eating biscuits and drawing moustaches on pictures in the previous day's *Daily Record*, it was left to me to deal with the guy.

Back up his ladders, the roofer spent several aggravating hours making loads more banging noises, making it really pretty difficult to concentrate on whether

Jordan would look funniest with a monocle, a bowler hat or a massive cigar.

There was very little in the way of interaction between us, the fellow paying me almost no mind whenever he had cause to traipse through the house to go back and forth to his van for tools. I got the sense he might have been unhappy with me, and wondered if this was due to my complete lack of hospitality: on principle, and against long-established social etiquette, I absolutely refuse to offer workmen a cup of tea.

My view is that if you like tea and don't have the initiative to bring a flask of your own with you to work, hard cheese. I'm not your mum.

This never goes down well, but if people in every other line of work can manage to sort their own refreshments, I'm sure the building trade could survive without their traditional raid on the teabag supplies of their customers.

'That should be you, son', announced the builder suddenly, appearing from the other room and startling me amidst my private moment of reflection on what useless tea-thieving bastards some folk were. 'I've sealed the lead flashing and that should be enough to stop it. Before I go, is it alright if I use the toilet?'

'Of course', I replied, thinking nothing of the innocuous request.

From that day on, my lack-of-own-tea-flask gripe has paled into absolute insignificance where the traits of workmen are concerned.

After an inordinately long time, the guy reappeared and with a small 'Thanks', took his white van and naffed off. Glad to have the house to myself again so I could laze about doing nothing in peace, I closed the front door and I...

Wonder what that UNGODLY smell is?!

Wow. What I thought was my builder spending a quick penny was obviously a grubby old man doing a big sit-down poo. No wonder he took so long.

Doesn't this break some blue-collar code? A slash is fine but surely a shit is out of bounds? Of course I wouldn't have okayed it had I known he was dropping kids off at the swimming pool.

Are we, as a society, really going to accept this? Can Britain ever really be Great, if its people go around shitting in each other's houses? For all our sakes, some things are best left to the confines of your own private domicile, and defecating is most definitely one of those things.

Two fingers up the nose still isn't enough as I scramble to light a candle and retreat like this is a World War II frontline.

I need a few hours just to recover.

Much later all's well – I've had a good lunch and I note, upon return to the scene of the crime, that the candle is all burned out.

There's no smell, but I do now notice some dirt marks on the floor. He's trailed something in. The stuff won't shift, and so there's now a black mark on my bathroom floor; this in addition to the smelly shit he's already taken it upon himself to dump in my lavatory. Talk about crossing a line.

Brilliant. Could he not have cleaned this himself?

I'm outraged. I sit down, ready myself for a wee jobby of my own, and ponder the state of Britain's manual labour industry. Builders running amok, bringing in muck and pooing in people's bathrooms. Not on, frankly. Not on!

But then...

'What?' I mutter, eyebrow raising to its peak height as I channel The Rock in his WWF prime.

What is this stuff on the underside of the toilet seat? There's a brown goo...

Some of it is touching my leg. It's touching my leg!

I cut my pee short as only possible in emergency

situations - a lorry headed your way as you piss by the side of the road, shouts of 'FIRE!' coming from outside your restroom cubicle or the sudden realisation that a mad axe-man has just burst into your house - and jump up like I'm spring-loaded.

'Surely...not...?' leaves my lips, as much to the builder himself (wherever he is at this point), as to myself and the room at large.

Like inspecting a potential suitcase bomb, as a final drop from my suddenly-terminated piss falls from the end of my penis onto my trousers, I cautiously lift the lid for a better look and instantly run through all the sanitary possibilities that explain this situation:

Perhaps he was eating a Nutella sandwich moments before using the toilet, and some spread has transferred from his hands to the seat.

Erm... at that, I'm done. What else could it be other than...?

I'm praying to God, to Allah, to the fat elephant (which, even by religious standards, I always thought was a little ridiculous), that the guy is a messy fan of choc sarnies. With all my might, I'm praying.

But the only way to guarantee peace of mind is to smell, and in a moment which I admit with hindsight could have been better thought through, I move in for a sniff...

Looking every inch like Kevin McCallister on a *Home Alone* poster, all I can manage to utter is: 'AAAAAAAAAAAAAAAAAAAARGH!'

As I'm stood there - trousers still at ankles, unsure whether to first wipe my own arse, clean my inner thigh or continue with the horrible job of ever-so-gingerly wet-wiping another man's faeces off my toilet seat, near crying like a rape victim - I stand back every now and again and utter the words 'What the fuck?' to the room at large in an increasingly irate and confused tone. Red faced, my sorrow turns to anger and my cries get louder: 'WHAT THE FUCK? WHAT THE ACTUAL FUCK?!'

The next day, following more heavy rainfall, the roof leaked again. Really, it's no wonder that he can't seal a roof when he can't even wipe his own arse properly, the grotty bastard.

Although I couldn't bring myself to explain why, I told my dad that that man wasn't setting foot in our house a third time and that I would rather we actually drowned than ever see him again. Bemused, Dad accepted this, and arranged for someone else to finally fix the roof once and for all.

One night soon after, as I lay unable to sleep for the persistent mental image of that Nutella-like atrocity that had grazed my inner thigh as I answered the call of nature, a horrible feeling struck me.

The ghost of a past memory eerily tickling my subconscious: was this karma?

Had whatever mysterious forces rule the universe decreed that this, this awful experience of becoming intimate with the contents of another man's bowel, was my penance for what had happened in that bathroom in Ireland?

I couldn't help but picture her then, that sweet, little, innocent, old woman whose bathroom I had laid waste to during the very worst of my chronic holiday diarrhea.

The hypocrisy of it all hit me. At least the builder was doing us a favour, albeit for financial recompense, and could claim some right to do with our toilet as he pleased: my dastardly dump was made worse by the fact that the woman had shown us all the kindness in the world. I repaid her by voiding my bowels in the worst way possible.

I tossed and turned some more in bed, reflecting that my childhood was truly done and dusted.

I pictured days spent fashioning hammocks in trees using cargo nets stolen from a fire station, or rolling a discarded bike tyre down a hilly road. I thought about staying up late to watch *Wrestlemania XVII*, that image of my hero The Rock lying helpless from chair shot after chair shot striking a chord with my current mood. I remembered those early days at secondary school, knuckling down for exam results not yet even a consideration; only food fights and games of Trippy-Uppy to concern myself with. I glumly ran through the lyrics to Lyle Lanley's song from *Marge vs. the Monorail* in my head, usually such a happy tune for me. I looked back on a day in which Thomas and I had been kicked out of his house while his mum cleaned; we spent the rest of that afternoon sitting on a grassy hill, absent-mindedly pulling daisies from the ground and talking shite to each other for hours, as the sun moved lazily across the sky.

All of those carefree times were behind me.

I was a man now; a man who paid other men to come into my house, make fruitless hammering noises, and leave faeces in their wake.

If this is the sort of thing that adulthood entails, I thought, I want to crawl back up into the womb of the 1990s and have that lovely, fluffy decade of Game Boy Colours and *Match* magazine and Noel Edmonds hold me in its warm embrace, and never let go.

ABOUT THE AUTHOR

What more do you want to know?! Isn't it enough that he's just shared some of his deepest, darkest secrets?! You already know that he once blew on his boner in the middle of Tesco. He's told you all about his most embarrassing toilet disaster, an awful onset of diarrhea in the middle of some stranger's house. He confessed to accidentally throwing a carrier bag full of shite into a field full of people. And we've just literally been over the fact that some grotty old man's faeces grazed the inside of his leg. Must you hound the man for more dirt?!

Fine. If you really have to know: Graeme was born on November 3rd, 1986. As a child, he took great delight in the fact that he shared a birthday with Josh Baskin, the main character in the film *Big* – something we learn in the scene where an adult-sized Josh is trying to convince his mother that it's really him.

He eats an unhealthy amount of cheese, recently added hits by Madonna, ABBA and Britney Spears to a Spotify playlist of his ultimate songs, and doesn't have any qualms whatsoever about wearing odd socks. His favourite part of being an altar boy was getting slipped a fiver for doing weddings and funerals. His favourite episode of *The Simpsons* is *Secrets of a Successful Marriage*.

Printed in Great Britain
by Amazon